UNIVERSITY CASEBOOK SERIES®

2019 SUPPLEMENT TO
BANKRUPTCY

TENTH EDITION

DANIEL J. BUSSEL
Professor of Law
University of California, Los Angeles

DAVID A. SKEEL, JR.
S. Samuel Arsht Professor of Corporate Law
University of Pennsylvania

MICHELLE M. HARNER
United States Bankruptcy Judge
District of Maryland

FOUNDATION
PRESS

University Casebook Series is a trademark registered in the U.S. Patent and Trademark Office.

© 2017, 2018 LEG, Inc. d/b/a West Academic
© 2019 LEG, Inc. d/b/a West Academic
    444 Cedar Street, Suite 700
    St. Paul, MN 55101
    1-877-888-1330

Printed in the United States of America

ISBN: 978-1-64242-938-1

PREFACE TO 2019 SUPPLEMENT TO TENTH EDITION

With this 2019 SUPPLEMENT, the Honorable Michelle M. Harner joins this Casebook as a co-author. Judge Harner was appointed to the United States Bankruptcy Court in the District of Maryland (Baltimore Division) in 2017. Prior to taking the bench, Judge Harner served with distinction on the law faculties of the University of Maryland Carey School of Law and the University of Nebraska, and as a partner at Jones Day LLP. We are proud to have her join us as a co-author of these materials.

Developments in the bankruptcy case law continue apace. The two most significant since the publication of the 2018 SUPPLEMENT are the Supreme Court's decisions in *Tempnology*, regarding the effect of rejection of trademark licenses, and *Taggart*, regarding enforcement of the bankruptcy discharge, both of which are reprinted in this 2019 SUPPLEMENT. In addition to these cases, and the updates set forth in earlier SUPPLEMENTS, we also note a variety of other developments since the publication of the TENTH EDITION for the convenience of both student and instructor.

Connor Meggs, UCLA School of Law Class of 2020, provided excellent research assistance for this 2019 SUPPLEMENT. Tal Grietzer, as usual, prepared the camera-ready manuscript of these materials. His great skill and care made timely publication of this 2019 SUPPLEMENT possible, and we are once again grateful for his efforts in our cause.

Daniel J. Bussel
UCLA School of Law
405 Hilgard Avenue
Los Angeles, CA 90095
bussel@law.ucla.edu
310-206-7977

David A. Skeel, Jr.
University of Pennsylvania
  Law School
3501 Sansom Street
Philadelphia, PA 19104
dskeel@law.upenn.edu
215-573-9859

Michelle M. Harner
US Bankruptcy Court
District of Maryland
Garmatz Federal Cthse
101 W. Lombard Street
Baltimore, MD 21201
410-962-2820

June 2019   D.J.B., D.A.S. & M.M.H.

i

SUMMARY OF CONTENTS

TABLE OF CONTENTS

TABLE OF CASES

The principal cases are in bold type.

UNIVERSITY CASEBOOK SERIES®

2019 SUPPLEMENT TO

BANKRUPTCY

TENTH EDITION

CHAPTER 1

INTRODUCTION

A. CONSENSUAL AND JUDICIAL LIENS

B. EARLY BANKRUPTCY LAW

C. OVERVIEW OF BANKRUPTCY

5. THE TRUSTEE IN BANKRUPTCY

> Following discussion of the U.S. Trustee system at p. 23 add:

Historically, the U.S. Trustee system has been funded by relatively modest U.S. Trustee fees calculated on quarterly disbursements by operating Chapter 11 debtors. 28 U.S.C. §1930(a)(6). Until 2017, the maximum fee was $30,000 per quarter imposed on debtors with over $30 million in quarterly disbursements. Estates with less than $15 million in quarterly disbursements paid no more than $13,000 per quarter. But in 2017, to the shock of most of the bankruptcy community, Congress passed the Bankruptcy Judgeship Act of 2017, Pub. L. No. 115-72, which for fiscal years 2018 through 2022 massively increased these fees should the U.S. Trustee System Fund balance fall below $200 million as of September 30 of the prior year. Under the new schedule, fees are set at the lesser of 1% of disbursements or $250,000 per quarter for all Chapter 11 debtors with more than $1 million in quarterly disbursements. The U.S. Trustee moreover has taken the position that these new larger fees are imposed on a per-debtor basis unless the estates have been substantively consolidated. Particularly in long-running multi-debtor operating Chapter 11 cases the new fee schedule represents a significant tax on the Chapter 11 process.

D. COMMENCEMENT OF BANKRUPTCY

> Following discussion of *Kingston Square*, p. 28 add:

In recent years, the so-called "Golden Share" has become a favored device for ensuring "bankruptcy remoteness." The "Golden Share" is a minority equity interest in the bankruptcy-remote entity held by the principal creditor or an affiliate of the principal creditor. The corporate charter or limited liability company operating agreement is drawn so the affirmative vote of the holder of the "Golden Share" is required to authorize a voluntary bankruptcy filing by the entity. In a widely discussed recent decision, *In re Intervention Energy Holdings, LLC*, 553 B.R. 258 (Bankr. D.Del. 2016), the Delaware bankruptcy court refused to enforce the "Golden Share" provision in the debtor's organizational documents on public policy grounds as an invalid waiver of bankruptcy rights. Subsequently, however, the Fifth Circuit, also applying Delaware law, has distinguished *Intervention Energy* and enforced such a provision, dismissing the bankruptcy filing as unauthorized without the consent of the holder of the Golden Share. *In re Franchise Services of North America, Inc.*, 891 F.3d 203 (5th Cir. 2018).

CHAPTER 2

THE BANKRUPTCY ESTATE

A. INTRODUCTION

2. DEFINING PROPERTY OF THE ESTATE

b. Divided Property Interests, Possession at Filing and Turnover

> Add to Note 3 following *Whiting Pools* at p. 38:

The issue of turnover of the consumer debtor's repossessed automobile continues to divide the courts. *Compare Denby-Peterson v. Nu2u Auto World*, 595 B.R. 184, 192 (D.N.J. 2018) (passive retention of vehicle not violation of §362(a)(3) of the Bankruptcy Code) *with In re Shannon*, 590 B.R. 467, 478 (Bankr. N.D. Ill. 2018) (finding automatic obligation to turn over vehicle under §542 and several violations of the automatic stay for creditor's failure to do so).

B. EXEMPT PROPERTY

CHAPTER 3

CLAIMS

A. INTRODUCTION

B. RIGHTS TO PAYMENT

1. LEGAL RIGHTS

> Insert on p. 87 at the end of **Note: Mass Future Claims in Bankruptcy**:

More recently, the limits on discharge of future liabilities were explored in connection with the "sale" of the assets of General Motors Corporation ("Old GM") to "New GM," pursuant to a bankruptcy sale orchestrated by the United States Government. In subsequent litigation, the Second Circuit found that the claims of future owners of vehicles manufactured by "Old GM" based on defective ignition switches remained potential liabilities of "New GM" notwithstanding the "free and clear" sale order entered by the bankruptcy court. *In re Motors Liquidation Co.*, 829 F.3d 135 (2d Cir. 2016), *cert. denied*, 137 S.Ct. 1813 (2017) (reprinted below in this 2019 SUPPLEMENT at p. 98).

2. EQUITABLE RIGHTS

> Insert on p. 90 as new Note 4:

Udell and its progeny are critiqued in the course of advocating for a multifactored balancing test that incorporates both bankruptcy and nonbankruptcy equities in determining when equitable remedies should be treated as bankruptcy "claims." *See* Daniel J. Bussel, *Doing Equity in Bankruptcy*, 34 EMORY BANKR. DEV. J. 13 (2018).

C. DETERMINING THE AMOUNT OF A CLAIM

D. SECURED CLAIMS

1. INTRODUCTION

2. VALUING A SECURED CLAIM

a. Cramdown

> Following *Rash*, p. 100:

In connection with the discussion of *Rash*, note the application of *Rash*'s valuation methodology in a Chapter 11 case in *In re Sunnyslope Housing LP*, 859 F.3d 637 (9th Cir. 2017) (en banc) (*as amended* June 23, 2017), *cert. denied,* 138 S. Ct. 648 (2018). An edited version of *Sunnyslope* is reprinted later in this 2019 SUPPLEMENT at p. 78 in connection with the Chapter 11 cramdown materials because of the interplay in *Sunnyslope* among its application of *Rash*, *Till* and §§1111(b) & 1129(b)(2)(A).

3. AVOIDING LIENS UNDER §506(d)

4. POSTFILING INTEREST ON SECURED CLAIMS

E. PRIORITY CLAIMS

CHAPTER 4

DISCHARGE

A. INTRODUCTION

B. DENIAL OF DISCHARGE BECAUSE OF DEBTOR'S MISCONDUCT

> Insert at p. 118 at the end of first sentence in third full
> paragraph of Section B:

See, e.g., In re Chlad, 922 F.3d 856 (7th Cir. 2019) (exploring the "knowingly and fraudulently" elements of §727(a)(4)).

C. NONDISCHARGEABLE DEBTS

1. UNSCHEDULED DEBTS

2. DOMESTIC SUPPORT OBLIGATIONS (DSO)

3. WILLFUL AND MALICIOUS INJURY

4. EDUCATIONAL LOANS

c. Federal Legislation

> Insert at p. 139 at the end of third full paragraph:

For a review of available income-based repayment plans and how courts should consider a debtor's use or non-use of such plans in the context of evaluating a debtor's request for a hardship discharge, *see* John Patrick Hunt, *Help or Hardship?: Income-Driven Repayment in Student-Loan Bankruptcies*, 106 GEO. L.J. 1278 (2018).

5. FRAUDULENTLY INCURRED DEBTS

> Insert at p. 140 at the end of Textual Note:

With respect to material misrepresentation of the debtor's financial condition, §523(a)(2) distinguishes between oral and written misrepresentations and makes creditor fraud claims based solely on oral misrepresentation dischargeable. *Lamar, Archer & Cofrin LLP v. Appling*, 138 S.Ct. 1752 (2018).

> Insert at p. 140 after Problem:

Husky Int'l Electronics, Inc. v. Ritz

Supreme Court of the United States, 2016.
136 S.Ct. 1581.

Justice SOTOMAYOR delivered the opinion of the Court.

The Bankruptcy Code prohibits debtors from discharging debts "obtained by ... false pretenses, a false representation, or actual fraud." 11 U.S.C. §523(a)(2)(A). The Fifth Circuit held that a debt is "obtained by ... actual fraud" only if the debtor's fraud involves a false representation to a creditor. That ruling deepened an existing split among the Circuits over whether "actual fraud" requires a false representation or whether it encompasses other traditional forms of fraud that can be accomplished without a false representation, such as a fraudulent conveyance of property made to evade payment to creditors. We granted *certiorari* to resolve that split and now reverse.

I

Husky International Electronics, Inc., is a Colorado-based supplier of components used in electronic devices. Between 2003 and 2007, Husky sold its products to Chrysalis Manufacturing Corp., and Chrysalis incurred a debt to Husky of $163,999.38. During the same period, respondent Daniel Lee Ritz, Jr., served as a director of Chrysalis and owned at least 30% of Chrysalis' common stock.

All parties agree that between 2006 and 2007, Ritz drained Chrysalis of assets it could have used to pay its debts to creditors like Husky by transferring large sums of Chrysalis' funds to other entities Ritz controlled. For instance— and Ritz' actions were by no means limited to these examples—Ritz transferred $52,600 to CapNet Risk Management, Inc., a company he owned in full; $121,831 to CapNet Securities Corp., a company in which he owned an 85% interest; and $99,386.90 to Dynalyst Manufacturing Corp., a company in which he owned a 25% interest.

In May 2009, Husky filed a lawsuit against Ritz seeking to hold him personally responsible for Chrysalis' $163,999.38 debt. Husky argued that Ritz' intercompany-transfer scheme was "actual fraud" for purposes of a Texas law that allows creditors to hold shareholders responsible for corporate debt. See Tex. Bus. Orgs. Code Ann. §21.223(b) (West 2012). In December 2009, Ritz filed for Chapter 7 bankruptcy in the United States Bankruptcy Court for the Southern District of Texas. Husky then initiated an adversarial proceeding in Ritz' bankruptcy case again seeking to hold Ritz personally liable for Chrysalis' debt. Husky also contended that Ritz could not discharge that debt in bankruptcy because the same intercompany-transfer scheme constituted "actual fraud" under 11 U.S.C. §523(a)(2)(A)'s exemption to discharge.[1]

---

[1] Husky also alleged that Ritz' debt should be exempted from discharge under two other exceptions, *see* 11 U.S.C. §523(a)(4) (excepting debts for fraud "while acting in a

The District Court held that Ritz was personally liable for the debt under Texas law, but that the debt was not "obtained by ... actual fraud" under §523(a)(2)(A) and could be discharged in his bankruptcy.

The Fifth Circuit affirmed. It did not address whether Ritz was responsible for Chrysalis' debt under Texas law because it agreed with the District Court that Ritz did not commit "actual fraud" under §523(a)(2)(A). Before the Fifth Circuit, Husky argued that Ritz' asset-transfer scheme was effectuated through a series of fraudulent conveyances—or transfers intended to obstruct the collection of debt. And, Husky said, such transfers are a recognizable form of "actual fraud." The Fifth Circuit disagreed, holding that a necessary element of "actual fraud" is a misrepresentation from the debtor to the creditor, as when a person applying for credit adds an extra zero to her income or falsifies her employment history. In transferring Chrysalis' assets, Ritz may have hindered Husky's ability to recover its debt, but the Fifth Circuit found that he did not make any false representations to Husky regarding those assets or the transfers and therefore did not commit "actual fraud."

We reverse. The term "actual fraud" in §523(a)(2)(A) encompasses forms of fraud, like fraudulent conveyance schemes, that can be effected without a false representation.

II

A

Before 1978, the Bankruptcy Code prohibited debtors from discharging debts obtained by "false pretenses or false representations." §35(a)(2) (1976 ed.). In the Bankruptcy Reform Act of 1978, Congress added "actual fraud" to that list. 92 Stat. 2590. The prohibition now reads: "A discharge under [Chapters 7, 11, 12, or 13] of this title does not discharge an individual debtor from any debt ... for money, property, services, or an extension, renewal, or refinancing of credit, to the extent obtained by ... false pretenses, a false representation, or actual fraud." §523(a)(2)(A) (2012 ed.).

When "'Congress acts to amend a statute, we presume it intends its amendment to have real and substantial effect.'" It is therefore sensible to start with the presumption that Congress did not intend "actual fraud" to mean the same thing as "a false representation," as the Fifth Circuit's holding suggests. But the historical meaning of "actual fraud" provides even stronger evidence that the phrase has long encompassed the kind of conduct alleged to have occurred here: a transfer scheme designed to hinder the collection of debt.

This Court has historically construed the terms in §523(a)(2)(A) to contain the "elements that the common law has defined them to include." *Field* v. *Mans* (US 1995). "Actual fraud" has two parts: actual and fraud. The word "actual" has a simple meaning in the context of common-law fraud: It denotes any fraud that "involv[es] moral turpitude or intentional wrong." *Neal* v. *Clark* (US 1878). "Actual" fraud stands in contrast to "implied" fraud or fraud "in law," which describe acts of deception that "may exist without the imputation of bad faith or immorality." Thus, anything that counts as "fraud" and is done with wrongful intent is "actual fraud."

---

fiduciary capacity"); §523(a)(6) (excepting debts for "willful and malicious injury"), but does not press those claims in this petition.

Although "fraud" connotes deception or trickery generally, the term is difficult to define more precisely. See 1 J. Story, Commentaries on Equity Jurisprudence §189 (6th ed. 1853) (Story) ("Fraud ... being so various in its nature, and so extensive in its application to human concerns, it would be difficult to enumerate all the instances in which Courts of Equity will grant relief under this head"). There is no need to adopt a definition for all times and all circumstances here because, from the beginning of English bankruptcy practice, courts and legislatures have used the term "fraud" to describe a debtor's transfer of assets that, like Ritz' scheme, impairs a creditor's ability to collect the debt.

One of the first bankruptcy acts, the Statute of 13 Elizabeth, has long been relied upon as a restatement of the law of so-called fraudulent conveyances (also known as "fraudulent transfers" or "fraudulent alienations"). See generally G. Glenn, The Law of Fraudulent Conveyances (1931). That statute, also called the Fraudulent Conveyances Act of 1571, identified as fraud "faigned covenous and fraudulent Feoffmentes Gyftes Grauntes Alienations [and] Conveyaunces" made with "Intent to delaye hynder or defraude Creditors." 13 Eliz. ch. 5. In modern terms, Parliament made it fraudulent to hide assets from creditors by giving them to one's family, friends, or associates. The principles of the Statute of 13 Elizabeth—and even some of its language—continue to be in wide use today. See *BFP v. Resolution Trust Corporation* (US 1994) ("The modern law of fraudulent transfers had its origin in the Statute of 13 Elizabeth"); *id.* ("Every American bankruptcy law has incorporated a fraudulent transfer provision"); Story §353 ("[T]he statute of 13 Elizabeth ... has been universally adopted in America, as the basis of our jurisprudence on the same subject"); *Boston Trading Group, Inc.* v. *Burnazos* (1st Cir 1987) (Breyer, J.) ("Mass. Gen. Laws ch. 109A, §§1–13 ... is a uniform state law that codifies both common and statutory law stretching back at least to 1571 and the Statute of Elizabeth"). The degree to which this statute remains embedded in laws related to fraud today clarifies that the common-law term "actual fraud" is broad enough to incorporate a fraudulent conveyance.

Equally important, the common law also indicates that fraudulent conveyances, although a "fraud," do not require a misrepresentation from a debtor to a creditor. As a basic point, fraudulent conveyances are not an inducement-based fraud. Fraudulent conveyances typically involve "a transfer to a close relative, a secret transfer, a transfer of title without transfer of possession, or grossly inadequate consideration." *BFP* (citing *Twyne's Case* (K. B. 1601)); O. Bump, Fraudulent Conveyances: A Treatise Upon Conveyances Made by Debtors To Defraud Creditors (3d ed. 1882)). In such cases, the fraudulent conduct is not in dishonestly inducing a creditor to extend a debt. It is in the acts of concealment and hindrance. In the fraudulent- conveyance context, therefore, the opportunities for a false representation from the debtor to the creditor are limited. The debtor may have the opportunity to put forward a false representation if the creditor inquires into the whereabouts of the debtor's assets, but that could hardly be considered a defining feature of this kind of fraud.

Relatedly, under the Statute of 13 Elizabeth and the laws that followed, both the debtor and the recipient of the conveyed assets were liable for fraud even though the recipient of a fraudulent conveyance of course made no representation, true or false, to the debtor's creditor. The famous *Twyne's Case*, which this Court relied upon in *BFP*, illustrates this point. See *Twyne's Case* (convicting Twyne of fraud under the Statute of 13 Elizabeth, even though he was the recipient of a debtor's conveyance). That principle underlies the now-common understanding that a "conveyance which hinders, delays or defrauds creditors shall be void as against [the recipient] unless ... th[at] party ... received it in good faith and for consideration." Glenn, Law of Fraudulent Conveyances §233. That principle also underscores the point that a false representation has never been a required element of "actual fraud," and we decline to adopt it as one today.

B

Ritz concedes that fraudulent conveyances are a form of "actual fraud,"[2] but contends that §523(a)(2)(A)'s particular use of the phrase means something else. Ritz' strained reading of the provision finds little support.

First, Ritz contends that interpreting "actual fraud" in §523(a)(2)(A) to encompass fraudulent conveyances would render duplicative two other exceptions to discharge in §523. Section 523(a)(4) exempts from discharge "any debt ... for fraud or defalcation while acting in a fiduciary capacity, embezzlement, or larceny." And §523(a)(6) exempts "any debt ... for willful and malicious injury by the debtor to another entity or to the property of another entity."

Ritz makes the unremarkable point that the traditional definition of "actual fraud" will cover some of the same conduct as those exceptions: for example, a trustee who fraudulently conveys away his trust's assets. But Ritz' interpretation does not avoid duplication, nor does our interpretation fail to preserve a meaningful difference between §523(a)(2)(A) and §§523(a)(4), (6). Just as a fiduciary who engages in a fraudulent conveyance may find his debt exempted from discharge under either §523(a)(2)(A) or §523(a)(4), so too would a fiduciary who engages in one of the fraudulent misrepresentations that form the core of Ritz' preferred interpretation of §523(a)(2)(A). The same is true for §523(a)(6). The debtors who commit fraudulent conveyances *and* the debtors who make false representations under §523(a)(2)(A) could likewise also inflict "willful and malicious injury" under §523(a)(6). There is, in short, overlap, but that overlap appears inevitable.

And, of course, our interpretation of "actual fraud" in §523(a)(2)(A) also preserves meaningful distinctions between that provision and §§523(a)(4), (a)(6). Section 523(a)(4), for instance, covers only debts for fraud while acting as a fiduciary, whereas §523(a)(2)(A) has no similar limitation. Nothing in our interpretation alters that distinction. And §523(a)(6) covers debts "for willful and malicious injury," whether or not that injury is the result of fraud, see *Kawaauhau* v. *Geiger* (US 1998) (discussing injuries resulting from "'intentional torts'"), whereas §523(a)(2)(A) covers only fraudulent acts. Nothing in our interpretation alters that distinction either. Thus, given the clear differences between these provisions, we see no reason to craft an artificial definition of "actual fraud" merely to avoid narrow redundancies in §523 that appear unavoidable.

Ritz also says that our interpretation creates redundancy with a separate section of the Bankruptcy Code, §727(a)(2), which prevents a debtor from discharging all of his debts if, within the year preceding the bankruptcy petition, he "transferred, removed, destroyed, mutilated, or concealed" property "with intent to hinder, delay, or defraud a creditor or an officer of the estate charged

---

[2] *See* Tr. of Oral Arg. 30 (JUSTICE KAGAN: "[Y]ou're not contesting that fraudulent conveyance is a form of actual fraud; is that right?" Ms. Murphy: "[Y]es, that's right"); *id.* (Ms. Murphy: "[T]o be clear, we don't dispute that fraudulent conveyance is a form of actual fraud").

with custody of property." Although the two provisions could cover some of the same conduct, they are meaningfully different. Section 727(a)(2) is broader than §523(a)(2)(A) in scope—preventing an offending debtor from discharging all debt in bankruptcy. But it is narrower than §523(a)(2)(A) in timing—applying only if the debtor fraudulently conveys assets in the year preceding the bankruptcy filing. In short, while §727(a)(2) is a blunt remedy for actions that hinder the entire bankruptcy process, §523(a)(2)(A) is a tailored remedy for behavior connected to specific debts.

Ritz' next point of resistance rests on §523(a)(2)(A)'s requirement that the relevant debt be "for money, property, services, or … credit … *obtained by* … actual fraud." (Emphasis added.) The argument, which the dissent also emphasizes, has two parts: First, it posits that fraudulent conveyances (unlike other forms of actual fraud) cannot be used to "obtai[n]" debt because they function instead to hide valuables that a debtor already possesses. There is, the dissent says, no debt at the end of a fraudulent conveyance that could be said to "'resul[t] from'" or be "'traceable to'" the fraud. Second, it urges that "actual fraud" not be interpreted to encompass forms of fraud that are incompatible with the provision's "obtained by" requirement.

It is of course true that the transferor does not "obtai[n]" debts in a fraudulent conveyance. But the recipient of the transfer—who, with the requisite intent, also commits fraud—can "obtai[n]" assets "by" his or her participation in the fraud. If that recipient later files for bankruptcy, any debts "traceable to" the fraudulent conveyance, see *Field*, will be nondischargable under §523(a)(2)(A). Thus, at least sometimes a debt "obtained by" a fraudulent conveyance scheme could be nondischargeable under §523(a)(2)(A). Such circumstances may be rare because a person who receives fraudulently conveyed assets is not necessarily (or even likely to be) a debtor on the verge of bankruptcy[3] but they make clear that fraudulent conveyances are not wholly incompatible with the "obtained by" requirement.

The dissent presses further still, contending that the phrase "obtained by … actual fraud" requires not only that the relevant debts "resul[t] from" or be "traceable to" fraud but also that they "result from fraud *at the inception of a credit transaction*." (emphasis added). Nothing in the text of §523(a)(2)(A) supports that additional requirement. The dissent bases its conclusion on this Court's opinion in *Field*, in which the Court noted that certain forms of bankruptcy fraud require a degree of direct reliance by a creditor on an action taken by a debtor. But *Field* discussed such "reliance" only in setting forth the requirements of the form of fraud alleged in that case—namely, fraud perpetrated through a misrepresentation to a creditor. The Court was not establishing a "reliance" requirement for frauds that are not premised on such a misrepresentation.

Finally, Ritz argues that Congress added the phrase "actual fraud" to §523(a)(2)(A) not to expand the exception's reach, but to restrict it. In Ritz' view, "actual fraud" was inserted as the last item in a disjunctive list—"false pretenses, a false representation, *or* actual fraud"—in order to make clear that

---

[3] Ritz' situation may be unusual in this regard because Husky contends that Ritz was both the transferor and the transferee in his fraudulent conveyance scheme, having transferred Chrysalis assets to other companies he controlled. We take no position on that contention here and leave it to the Fifth Circuit to decide on remand whether the debt to Husky was "obtained by" Ritz' asset-transfer scheme.

the "false pretenses" and "false representation[s]" covered by the provision needed to be intentional. Ritz asks us, in other words, to ignore what he believes is Congress' "imprudent use of the word 'or,'" and read the final item in the list to modify and limit the others. In essence, he asks us to change the word "or" to "by." That is an argument that defeats itself. We can think of no other example, nor could petitioner point to any at oral argument, in which this Court has attempted such an unusual statutory modification.

* * *

Because we must give the phrase "actual fraud" in §523(a)(2)(A) the meaning it has long held, we interpret "actual fraud" to encompass fraudulent conveyance schemes, even when those schemes do not involve a false representation. We therefore reverse the judgment of the Fifth Circuit and remand the case for further proceedings consistent with this opinion.

So ordered.

Justice THOMAS, dissenting.

[Omitted].

6.   FRAUD AND DEFALCATION

> Add to the end of Textual Note at pp. 140-41:

Bullock v. BankChampaign, N.A., 569 U.S. 267 (2013) resolved the split in the circuits regarding the meaning of the statutory term "defalcation" by adopting the view that the exception to discharge requires a culpable state of mind on the part of the defalcating debtor.

7.   CREDIT CARD FRAUD

8.   FINE, PENALTY OR FORFEITURE

    a.   Punitive Damages

    b.   Criminal Penalties

> Add to the end of Textual Note at pp. 147-48:

Abbye Atkinson, *Consumer Bankruptcy, Nondischargeability, and Penal Debt*, 70 VAND. L. REV. 97 (2017) critiques the penal debt exception to discharge from a policy perspective.

    c.   Restitution Settlements

9.   TAXES

D. PROTECTION OF THE DISCHARGE

1. INTRODUCTION

> Insert at p. 151 at the end of Section D.1:

Although §524 does not expressly provide for sanctions against a creditor who violates the discharge injunction, courts generally invoke their contempt powers to address such conduct. In the case that follows, the Supreme Court evaluates whether a creditor's good faith belief that the discharge is not applicable to its debt protects the creditor from contempt sanctions for an alleged violation of the discharge injunction.

Taggart v. Lorenzen

Supreme Court of the United States, 2019.
2019 U.S. LEXIS 3890.

BREYER, J., delivered the opinion for a unanimous Court.

At the conclusion of a bankruptcy proceeding, a bankruptcy court typically enters an order releasing the debtor from liability for most prebankruptcy debts. This order, known as a discharge order, bars creditors from attempting to collect any debt covered by the order. See 11 U. S. C. §524(a)(2). The question presented here concerns the criteria for determining when a court may hold a creditor in civil contempt for attempting to collect a debt that a discharge order has immunized from collection.

The Bankruptcy Court, in holding the creditors here in civil contempt, applied a standard that it described as akin to "strict liability" based on the standard's expansive scope. … It held that civil contempt sanctions are permissible, irrespective of the creditor's beliefs, so long as the creditor was "'aware of the discharge'" order and "'intended the actions which violate[d]'" it. … The Court of Appeals for the Ninth Circuit, however, disagreed with that standard. Applying a subjective standard instead, it concluded that a court cannot hold a creditor in civil contempt if the creditor has a "good faith belief" that the discharge order "does not apply to the creditor's claim." … That is so, the Court of Appeals held, "even if the creditor's belief is unreasonable." …

We conclude that neither a standard akin to strict liability nor a purely subjective standard is appropriate. Rather, in our view, a court may hold a creditor in civil contempt for violating a discharge order if there is *no fair ground of doubt* as to whether the order barred the creditor's conduct. In other words, civil contempt may be appropriate if there is no objectively reasonable basis for concluding that the creditor's conduct might be lawful.

I

Bradley Taggart, the petitioner, formerly owned an interest in an Oregon company, Sherwood Park Business Center. That company, along with two of its other owners, brought a lawsuit in Oregon state court, claiming that Taggart had breached the Business Center's operating agreement. (We use the name "Sherwood" to refer to the company, its two owners, and—in some instances— their former attorney, who is now represented by the executor of his estate. The company, the two owners, and the executor are the respondents in this case.)

Before trial, Taggart filed for bankruptcy under Chapter 7 of the Bankruptcy Code, which permits insolvent debtors to discharge their debts by liquidating assets to pay creditors. ... Ultimately, the Federal Bankruptcy Court wound up the proceeding and issued an order granting him a discharge. Taggart's discharge order, like many such orders, goes no further than the statute: It simply says that the debtor "shall be granted a discharge under §727." ... Section 727, the statute cited in the discharge order, states that a discharge relieves the debtor "from all debts that arose before the date of the order for relief[.]" ... The words of the discharge order, though simple, have an important effect: A discharge order "operates as an injunction" that bars creditors from collecting any debt that has been discharged. ...

After the issuance of Taggart's federal bankruptcy discharge order, the Oregon state court proceeded to enter judgment against Taggart in the prebankruptcy suit involving Sherwood. Sherwood then filed a petition in state court seeking attorney's fees that were incurred *after* Taggart filed his bankruptcy petition. All parties agreed that, under the Ninth Circuit's decision in *In re Ybarra*, 424 F. 3d 1018 (2005), a discharge order would normally cover and thereby discharge postpetition attorney's fees stemming from prepetition litigation (such as the Oregon litigation) *unless* the discharged debtor "'returned to the fray'" after filing for bankruptcy. ... Sherwood argued that Taggart had "returned to the fray" postpetition and therefore was liable for the postpetition attorney's fees that Sherwood sought to collect. The state trial court agreed and held Taggart liable for roughly $45,000 of Sherwood's postpetition attorney's fees.

At this point, Taggart returned to the Federal Bankruptcy Court. He argued that he had not returned to the state-court "fray" under *Ybarra*, and that the discharge order therefore barred Sherwood from collecting postpetition attorney's fees. Taggart added that the court should hold Sherwood in civil contempt because Sherwood had violated the discharge order. The Bankruptcy Court did not agree. It concluded that Taggart had returned to the fray. Finding no violation of the discharge order, it refused to hold Sherwood in civil contempt.

Taggart appealed, and the Federal District Court held that Taggart had not returned to the fray. Hence, it concluded that Sherwood violated the discharge order by trying to collect attorney's fees. The District Court remanded the case to the Bankruptcy Court.

The Bankruptcy Court, noting the District Court's decision, then held Sherwood in civil contempt. In doing so, it applied a standard it likened to "strict liability." ... The Bankruptcy Court held that civil contempt sanctions were appropriate because Sherwood had been "'aware of the discharge'" order and "'intended the actions which violate[d]'" it. ... The court awarded Taggart approximately $105,000 in attorney's fees and costs, $5,000 in damages for emotional distress, and $2,000 in punitive damages.

Sherwood appealed. The Bankruptcy Appellate Panel vacated these sanctions, and the Ninth Circuit affirmed the panel's decision. The Ninth Circuit applied a very different standard than the Bankruptcy Court. It concluded that a "creditor's good faith belief" that the discharge order "does not apply to the creditor's claim precludes a finding of contempt, even if the creditor's belief is unreasonable." ... Because Sherwood had a "good faith belief" that the discharge order "did not apply" to Sherwood's claims, the Court of Appeals held that civil contempt sanctions were improper. ...

Taggart filed a petition for certiorari, asking us to decide whether "a creditor's good-faith belief that the discharge injunction does not apply precludes a finding of civil contempt." … We granted certiorari.

II

The question before us concerns the legal standard for holding a creditor in civil contempt when the creditor attempts to collect a debt in violation of a bankruptcy discharge order. Two Bankruptcy Code provisions aid our efforts to find an answer. The first, section 524, says that a discharge order "operates as an injunction against the commencement or continuation of an action, the employment of process, or an act, to collect, recover or offset" a discharged debt. 11 U. S. C. §524(a)(2). The second, section 105, authorizes a court to "issue any order, process, or judgment that is necessary or appropriate to carry out the provisions of this title." §105(a).

In what circumstances do these provisions permit a court to hold a creditor in civil contempt for violating a discharge order? In our view, these provisions authorize a court to impose civil contempt sanctions when there is no objectively reasonable basis for concluding that the creditor's conduct might be lawful under the discharge order.

A

Our conclusion rests on a longstanding interpretive principle: When a statutory term is "'obviously transplanted from another legal source,'" it "'brings the old soil with it.'" … Here, the statutes specifying that a discharge order "operates as an injunction," §524(a)(2), and that a court may issue any "order" or "judgment" that is "necessary or appropriate" to "carry out" other bankruptcy provisions, §105(a), bring with them the "old soil" that has long governed how courts enforce injunctions.

That "old soil" includes the "potent weapon" of civil contempt. [*Philadelphia Marine Trade Assn.*, 389 U. S. at 76.] Under traditional principles of equity practice, courts have long imposed civil contempt sanctions to "coerce the defendant into compliance" with an injunction or "compensate the complainant for losses" stemming from the defendant's noncompliance with an injunction. [*Mine Workers*, 330 U. S. at 303–304.]

The bankruptcy statutes, however, do not grant courts unlimited authority to hold creditors in civil contempt. Instead, as part of the "old soil" they bring with them, the bankruptcy statutes incorporate the traditional standards in equity practice for determining when a party may be held in civil contempt for violating an injunction. In cases outside the bankruptcy context, we have said that civil contempt "should not be resorted to where there is [a] *fair ground of doubt* as to the wrongfulness of the defendant's conduct." [*Molitor*, 113 U. S. at 618.] This standard reflects the fact that civil contempt is a "severe remedy," *ibid.*, and that principles of "basic fairness requir[e] that those enjoined receive explicit notice" of "what conduct is outlawed" before being held in civil contempt, *Schmidt v. Lessard*, 414 U. S. 473, 476 (1974) (*per curiam*). …

This standard is generally an *objective* one. We have explained before that a party's subjective belief that she was complying with an order ordinarily will not insulate her from civil contempt if that belief was objectively unreasonable. As we said in *McComb* v. *Jacksonville Paper Co.*, 336 U. S. 187 (1949), "[t]he absence of wilfulness does not relieve from civil contempt." …

We have not held, however, that subjective intent is always irrelevant. Our cases suggest, for example, that civil contempt sanctions may be warranted when a party acts in bad faith. ... Thus, in *McComb*, we explained that a party's "record of continuing and persistent violations" and "persistent contumacy" justified placing "the burden of any uncertainty in the decree ... on [the] shoulders" of the party who violated the court order. 336 U. S., at 192–193. On the flip side of the coin, a party's good faith, even where it does not bar civil contempt, may help to determine an appropriate sanction. ...

These traditional civil contempt principles apply straightforwardly to the bankruptcy discharge context. The typical discharge order entered by a bankruptcy court is not detailed. ... Congress, however, has carefully delineated which debts are exempt from discharge. See §§523(a)(1)–(19). Under the fair ground of doubt standard, civil contempt therefore may be appropriate when the creditor violates a discharge order based on an objectively unreasonable understanding of the discharge order or the statutes that govern its scope.

B

[The Court begins this Section by rejecting the Ninth Circuit's subjective standard as, among other things, being "inconsistent with traditional civil contempt principles, under which parties cannot be insulated from a finding of civil contempt based on their subjective good faith."]

Taggart, meanwhile, argues for a standard like the one applied by the Bankruptcy Court. This standard would permit a finding of civil contempt if the creditor was aware of the discharge order and intended the actions that violated the order. ... Because most creditors are aware of discharge orders and intend the actions they take to collect a debt, this standard would operate much like a strict-liability standard. It would authorize civil contempt sanctions for a violation of a discharge order regardless of the creditor's subjective beliefs about the scope of the discharge order, and regardless of whether there was a reasonable basis for concluding that the creditor's conduct did not violate the order. Taggart argues that such a standard would help the debtor obtain the "fresh start" that bankruptcy promises. He adds that a standard resembling strict liability would be fair to creditors because creditors who are unsure whether a debt has been discharged can head to federal bankruptcy court and obtain an advance determination on that question before trying to collect the debt. ...

We doubt, however, that advance determinations would provide a workable solution to a creditor's potential dilemma. A standard resembling strict liability may lead risk-averse creditors to seek an advance determination in bankruptcy court even where there is only slight doubt as to whether a debt has been discharged. And because discharge orders are written in general terms and operate against a complex statutory backdrop, there will often be at least some doubt as to the scope of such orders. Taggart's proposal thus may lead to frequent use of the advance determination procedure. Congress, however, expected that this procedure would be needed in only a small class of cases. ... The widespread use of this procedure also would alter who decides whether a debt has been discharged, moving litigation out of state courts, which have concurrent jurisdiction over such questions, and into federal courts. ...

Taggart's proposal would thereby risk additional federal litigation, additional costs, and additional delays. That result would interfere with "a chief purpose of the bankruptcy laws": "'to secure a prompt and effectual'" resolution of bankruptcy cases " 'within a limited period.'" [*Landy*, 382 U. S. at 328.] These negative consequences, especially the costs associated with the added need to appear in federal proceedings, could work to the disadvantage of debtors as well as creditors.

Taggart also notes that lower courts often have used a standard akin to strict liability to remedy violations of automatic stays. ... An automatic stay is entered at the outset of a bankruptcy proceeding. The statutory provision that addresses the remedies for violations of automatic stays says that "an individual injured by any willful violation" of an automatic stay "shall recover actual damages, including costs and attorneys' fees, and, in appropriate circumstances, may recover punitive damages." 11 U. S. C. §362(k)(1). This language, however, differs from the more general language in section 105(a). ... The purposes of automatic stays and discharge orders also differ: A stay aims to prevent damaging disruptions to the administration of a bankruptcy case in the short run, whereas a discharge is entered at the end of the case and seeks to bind creditors over a much longer period. These differences in language and purpose sufficiently undermine Taggart's proposal to warrant its rejection. (We note that the automatic stay provision uses the word "willful," a word the law typically does not associate with strict liability but "'whose construction is often dependent on the context in which it appears.' " [Burr, 551 U. S. at 57.] We need not, and do not, decide whether the word "willful" supports a standard akin to strict liability.)

III

We conclude that the Court of Appeals erred in applying a subjective standard for civil contempt. Based on the traditional principles that govern civil contempt, the proper standard is an objective one. A court may hold a creditor in civil contempt for violating a discharge order where there is not a "fair ground of doubt" as to whether the creditor's conduct might be lawful under the discharge order. In our view, that standard strikes the "careful balance between the interests of creditors and debtors" that the Bankruptcy Code often seeks to achieve. [Rameker, 573 U. S. at 129.]

Because the Court of Appeals did not apply the proper standard, we vacate the judgment below and remand the case for further proceedings consistent with this opinion.

It is so ordered.

2. DISCHARGE EXCEPTIONS PROCEDURES

E. DISCRIMINATION AGAINST DEBTORS

CHAPTER 5

STAYS AND INJUNCTIONS

A. INTRODUCTION

B. APPLICABILITY OF THE STAY

C. EFFECT OF VIOLATION OF STAY

D. SECURED CLAIMS

> Insert at the end of Problem, pp. 183-84:

See also In re 1075 S. Yukon, LLC, 590 B.R. 527 (Bankr. D. Colo. 2018) (holding that exercise of an option to purchase real estate was not "any other similar act" under §108(b) and therefore refusing to extend Debtor's right to exercise the option beyond contractual expiration date).

E. ACTIONS AGAINST NONDEBTORS

> Insert at the end of Note 2, p. 191:

But *see Martinez v. OGA Charters, LLC (In re Charters LLC)*, 901 F.3d 599 (5th Cir. 2018), in which the court applied the *Edgeworth* framework to a case where $400 million in claims from a multitude of tort plaintiffs far exceeded the $5 million liability policy limit. The court held that the policy proceeds were properly classified as property of the bankruptcy estate in order to equitably distribute insufficient insurance proceeds among eligible competing claimants.

F. RELIEF FROM AUTOMATIC STAY FOR CAUSE

G. RELIEF FROM STAY AND ADEQUATE PROTECTION RIGHTS FOR UNDERSECURED CREDITORS

> After Note: Single Asset Real Estate, pp. 209-10 add:

The SARE debtor's ability to use rents to satisfy adequate protection requirements has been thrown into doubt by the following decision of the Sixth Circuit, which uses state law to characterize encumbered rents that would otherwise appear to be cash collateral under §§363(a), (c), 552(b) as property of the mortgagee:

In re Town Center Flats, LLC

United States Court of Appeals, Sixth Circuit, 2017.
855 F.3d 721 *cert. denied* 138 S.Ct. 328.

■ JANE B. STRANCH, Circuit Judge.

This bankruptcy case centers on property rights in an assigned stream of rents. The extent of a debtor's rights in those rents under Michigan law determines whether the rents are properly included in a Chapter 11 bankruptcy estate. The bankruptcy court decided that an assignment of rents creates a security interest, but does not change ownership, and held that an assignor continues to have a property interest in the rents. Accordingly, the bankruptcy court included the rents in the bankruptcy estate. The district court vacated the order of the bankruptcy court, finding that an assignment of rents is a transfer of ownership under Michigan law and thus the rents should not be included in the bankruptcy estate. Agreeing with the district court's reasoning, we hold that the debtor, Town Center Flats, LLC, did not retain sufficient rights in the assigned rents under Michigan law for those rents to be included in the bankruptcy estate. We therefore **reverse** the order of the bankruptcy court.

I. BACKGROUND

A. Factual History

The parties do not dispute the underlying facts. Debtor Town Center Flats, LLC owns a 53-unit residential complex in Shelby Township, Michigan. Town Center financed construction of the building with a $5.3 million loan from Key-Bank that was later assigned to ECP Commercial II LLC. The loan was secured with a mortgage and an agreement to assign rents to the creditor in the event of default. In the agreement to assign rents, Town Center "irrevocably, absolutely and unconditionally [agreed to] transfer, sell, assign, pledge and convey to Assignee, its successors and assigns, all of the right, title and interest of [Town Center] in … income of every nature of and from the Project, including, without limitation, minimum rents [and] additional rents…." The agreement purported to be a "present, absolute and executed grant of the powers herein granted to Assignee," while simultaneously granting a license to Town Center to collect and retain rents until an event of default, at which point the license would "automatically terminate without notice to [Town Center]." Rents from the residential complex are Town Center's only source of income.

On December 31, 2013, Town Center defaulted on its obligation to repay the loan. On December 22, 2014, ECP sent a notice of default and a request for the payment of rents to all known tenants of the Town Center property. The notice complied with the terms of the agreement and with Mich. Comp. Laws §554.231, which allows creditors to collect rents directly from tenants of certain mortgaged properties. The following day, ECP recorded the notice documents in Macomb County, Michigan, completing the last step required by the statute to make the assignment of rents binding against both Town Center and the tenants of the property.

On January 23, 2015, ECP filed a complaint in the Circuit Court for Macomb County alleging breach of contract, initiating foreclosure on the mortgage, and requesting appointment of a receiver to take possession of the Town Center property. Approximately one week later on January 31, 2015, Town Center filed for Chapter 11 bankruptcy relief. At the time Town Center filed its petition, Town Center owed ECP $5,329,329 plus attorney's fees and costs.

The parties have reached an interim agreement to allow Town Center to continue to collect rents from the tenants of the complex, with $15,000 per month used to pay down the debt to ECP and the remainder of the rents used for authorized expenses.

B. Procedural History

Town Center's bankruptcy petition resulted in an automatic stay on the state-court case filed by ECP. *See* 11 U.S.C. §362(a) (placing a stay on most judicial actions involving the debtor when a bankruptcy petition is filed). In February 2015, ECP filed a motion to prohibit Town Center from using rents collected after the petition was filed. Town Center opposed the motion and pointed out to the bankruptcy court that the company would have no income to work with in its Chapter 11 reorganization plan if the rents were not part of the bankruptcy estate. The bankruptcy court agreed with Town Center and denied ECP's motion. The bankruptcy court determined that the assigned rents would qualify as cash collateral in the bankruptcy estate, meaning, under Chapter 11, that Town Center must provide "adequate protection" to ECP before using the cash. *In re Buttermilk Towne Ctr., LLC* (B.A.P. 6th Cir. 2010).

ECP appealed to the district court and argued that Michigan law established a transfer of ownership in the assigned rents from Town Center to ECP. The district court agreed with ECP and vacated the bankruptcy court's decision. Town Center appealed to this court. ECP moved to dismiss the appeal for lack of jurisdiction, arguing that the decisions of the lower courts were not final because the bankruptcy case is still open. A motions panel of this court decided that additional proceedings in the bankruptcy court would be purely ministerial and that we have jurisdiction over an appeal from a final order. We therefore reach the merits to decide whether the assigned rents are property of ECP or are part of Town Center's bankruptcy estate.

II. ANALYSIS

A. Standard of Review and Applicable Law

...

Property rights are determined under the law of the state in which the real property is located, which in this case is Michigan. Using state law to define rights promotes the "[u]niform treatment of property interests by both state and federal courts," which serves to "reduce uncertainty, to discourage forum shopping, and to prevent a party from receiving 'a windfall merely by reason of the happenstance of bankruptcy.'" *Butner v. United States* (US 1979). When the highest court of a state has not spoken directly on an issue, this court must make an *Erie* guess as to how that court would resolve it and may look to decisions of intermediate state appellate courts as persuasive authority. Once property rights have been determined under state law, "federal bankruptcy law dictates to what extent that interest is property of the estate." *Bavely v. United States (In re Terwillinger's Catering Plus, Inc.)* (6th Cir. 1990).

We begin by analyzing the extent of property rights held by the assignor and assignee of rents under Michigan law. We then answer the ultimate question—whether the rights retained by the assignor are sufficient for those rents to be included in the bankruptcy estate.

B. Assignment of Rents in Michigan

As with many issues of property rights, the history of the legal doctrine sheds light on the traditional legal rule, which serves to illuminate more recent developments. The traditional rule in Michigan, created by statute in 1843, was that an assignment of rents was unenforceable because it would interfere with a mortgagor's right of redemption. *Smith v. Mut. Ben. Life Ins. Co.* (Mich. 1960). The default rule in Michigan is therefore that an assignment of rents is unenforceable. A 1925 statute subsequently created a right to assign rents for properties subject to trust mortgages. The Michigan Supreme Court determined that the statute made the "[c]ollection of rents ... not merely an incident to the right of possession of the land, but ... a distinct remedy and additional security." *Security Trust Co. v. Sloman* (Mich. 1930). Central to this case, a 1953 statute titled "Assignment of Rents to Accrue from Leases as Additional Mortgage Security" extended the ability to assign rents to additional categories of property:

> Hereafter, in or in connection with any mortgage on commercial or industrial property ... it shall be lawful to assign the rents, or any portion thereof, under any oral or written leases upon the mortgaged property to the mortgagee, as security in addition to the property described in such mortgage. Such assignment of rents shall be binding upon such assignor only in the event of default in the terms and conditions of said mortgage, and shall operate against and be binding upon the occupiers of the premises from the date of filing by the mortgagee in the office of the register of deeds for the county in which the property is located of a notice of default in the terms and conditions of the mortgage and service of a copy of such notice upon the occupiers of the mortgaged premises.

Mich. Comp. Laws §554.231.

The Michigan statute also contains a provision about the validity of the assignment:

> The assignment of rents, when so made, shall be a good and valid assignment of the rents to accrue under any lease or leases in existence or coming into existence during the period the mortgage is in effect, against the mortgagor or mortgagors or those claiming under or through them from the date of the recording of such mortgage, and shall be binding upon the tenant under the lease or leases upon service of a copy of the instrument under which the assignment is made, together with notice of default as required by [the above section].

Id. §554.232.

1. Assignment of Rents

Michigan courts generally discuss assignments of rents under §554.231 as ownership transfers. The Michigan Supreme Court held that this statute puts the assignee "in the shoes of the mortgagor until the debt is paid, with all his rights to the rents and profits as long as he, under the general law of mortgages, could enjoy them." In 1994, the Michigan Court of Appeals held that a prior-perfected interest in assigned rents had priority over an interest held by a judgment creditor who sought to garnish rents. *Otis Elevator Co. v. Mid-America Realty Investors* (Mich. Ct. App. 1994). The judgment creditor "could not garnish rents because [the assignor] no longer had an interest in the rents." Once an assignee has: 1) entered into an agreement to assign rents; 2) recorded that agreement; and 3) default has occurred, then the assignee's rights "are perfected and binding against the assignor" and the assignor "no longer ha[s] a valid property interest in the rents." The assignor has the legal right to collect the rents directly from tenants once notice of the default has been filed in the county's register and served on the tenants. Mich. Comp. Laws §§554.231, 554.232. Michigan courts have generally treated the assignment of rents as a transfer of ownership once the agreement has been completed and recorded and a default has occurred. *See Otis Elevator* (stating "once [the assignee] recorded the mortgage and the mortgagor's default, the assignment of rents was valid and enforceable as between the mortgagor ... and the mortgagee."). *Otis Elevator* implies that this should be regarded as a transfer of all rights in the rents. *Id.* (finding that the assignor "no longer had an interest in the rents."). A more recent decision of the Michigan Court of Appeals confirmed that the assignor loses "any right to collect the rents" after the assignee has perfected its rights following an event of default. *Ashley Livonia A&P, L.L.C. v. Great Atl. & Pac. Tea Co., Inc.*, No. 319288 (Mich. Ct. App. June 16, 2015) (per curiam). We therefore predict, under *Erie v. Tompkins*, that the Michigan Supreme Court would treat a completed assignment of rents as a transfer of ownership.

Town Center argues that the title and language of the Michigan statute make it clear that only a security interest, not an ownership interest, is assigned under this law. Section 554.231 is titled "Assignment of Rents to Accrue as Additional Mortgage Security" and the body of the statute says "it shall be lawful to assign the rents ... as security in addition to the property described in [the] mortgage." Town Center would have us read the statute as expressing the Michigan legislature's intention to allow only transfers of security interests, and not ownership, based on its language authorizing assignments "as security in addition to the property." Mich. Comp. Laws §554.231. Town Center reasons that the statute allows only for a security interest in the assigned rents, so any attempt to transfer ownership of the rents is blocked by the default rule that an assignment of rents is unenforceable.

Language that the assignment is "as security," however, does not foreclose an ownership transfer. For example, a deed of trust transfers a deed—which is commonly thought of as an ownership transfer—to a trustee to hold as security for obligations associated with a mortgage on the property. And Michigan courts have consistently read §554.231 as allowing for assignments of rents to be transfers of ownership once the statutory steps for perfection have been completed. We follow their lead in interpreting the language of §554.231 as allowing for ownership interests to be transferred with an assignment of rents.

In the agreement at issue in this case, Town Center used broad language to "irrevocably, absolutely and unconditionally" transfer its right in a "present, absolute and executed assignment of the Rents and of the Leases" from the Town Center property. The only fair reading of this language is that Town Center assigned the rents to the maximum extent permitted by Michigan law. Because we hold that Mich. Comp. Laws §554.231 allows for an ownership transfer in these circumstances, we find that Town Center did transfer ownership in the assigned rents to ECP before the bankruptcy petition was filed in this case. The broad language of the agreement evidences an intention to transfer ownership.

2. Residual Rights of Assignor

Even with a transfer of ownership under §554.231, Town Center argues that it retains some rights in the rents under Michigan law. If an assignor cures the default according to the agreement's terms, then the assignor is able to start collecting rents again. *See Sloman* (noting, under the analogous 1925 statute, that "the purpose of the act is to put the [assignee] in the shoes of the [assignor] *until the debt is paid.*" (emphasis added)). Town Center reasons that if the rents from the property are thought of as a stream of money, Town Center continues to hold a contingent future interest in collecting those rents. The future interest is realized if and when Town Center cures the default. On the other hand, if the rents are thought of as payments that occur during the discrete time period between the event of default and a (potential) future cure, then ECP has the sole interest in those payments and Town Center has no interest in them. This holds true even if Town Center later cures the default. We find the latter conceptualization of a discrete period to be more aligned with the text of the statute. *See* Mich. Comp. Laws §554.232 (creating right to assign "rents to accrue … during the period the mortgage is in effect").

Town Center also points to a second residual right: Michigan courts have created restrictions on how the assignee can use rents collected under the law. In *Smith*, the court filled in the "obviously intended requirement that rents collected by the [assignee] shall be applied on the mortgage debt." The court approved use of the collected rents to pay the debt, property taxes, and insurance policy premiums. Neither the Michigan Supreme Court nor the Michigan Court of Appeals has concluded that these restrictions on the assignee's use of rent money create a property right vested in the assignor. We decline to create a new rule of Michigan property law on this issue, especially because such a rule would conflict with language used by Michigan appellate courts. *See Otis Elevator* (concluding that the assignor "no longer had an interest in the rents").

In summary, Michigan law treats a completed assignment of rents as a change of ownership and the assignor of those rents does not retain residual property rights in the assigned rents.

C. Scope of Bankruptcy Estates under the Federal Bankruptcy Code

Federal law determines the scope of the bankruptcy estate, which is broad. The Supreme Court has explained that "[b]oth the congressional goal of encouraging reorganizations and Congress' choice of methods to protect secured creditors suggest that Congress intended a broad range of property to be included in the estate." *United States v. Whiting Pools, Inc.* (US 1983). In *Whiting Pools*, personal property that had been seized by the Internal Revenue Service under a tax lien was determined to be part of the bankruptcy estate. The Court found that the IRS had a secured interest in the property, but that the debtor still retained an ownership interest until sale to a bona fide purchaser at a tax sale. *Id.* A broad definition of the bankruptcy estate was in line with the congressional intent to allow Chapter 11 reorganization so "the business would continue to provide jobs, to satisfy creditors' claims, and to produce a return for its owners." *Id.* (quoting H.R. Rep. No. 95-595, p. 220 (1977)).

Despite the broad scope of Chapter 11 bankruptcy estates, the assigned rents in this case are not properly included in the Town Center estate. As discussed above, Town Center does not retain ownership of the rents and does not hold residual property rights in those rents. Instead, the rents belong to ECP. Our holding is in line with the majority of bankruptcy court decisions that have addressed this issue. In 1992, a bankruptcy court in the Western District of Michigan held that assigned rents under Mich. Comp. Laws §554.231 were not part of the bankruptcy estate because the debtor maintained only an inchoate right to future rents. *In re Mount Pleasant Ltd. P'ship* (Bankr. W.D. Mich. 1992). A recent decision from the Eastern District of Michigan agreed that assigned rents are property of the assignee, not part of the bankruptcy estate. *In re Madison Heights Grp., LLC* (Bankr. E.D. Mich. 2014). A bankruptcy court in the Southern District of New York, interpreting §554.231, reached a similar conclusion, finding the language in *Otis Elevator* to be especially persuasive. *In re Woodmere Inv'rs Ltd. P'ship* (Bankr. S.D.N.Y. 1995).

The bankruptcy court in this case relied on its own previous opinion that came to the opposite conclusion. These two decisions were motivated by a policy concern that excluding the assigned rents from the estate would effectively foreclose Chapter 11 relief for companies like Town Center that own a single property and receive their sole stream of revenue from rents of that property. We recognize the concern of Town Center—and the bankruptcy court—that single-asset real estate entities may have limited options under Chapter 11 in this situation. Michigan law, however, is clear on the matter and governs despite other policy concerns.

III. CONCLUSION

Mich. Comp. Laws §554.231 allows for transfers of ownership when an agreement to assign rents indicates an intention to do that, has been recorded, and default has occurred. Because Town Center does not have rights under Michigan law in the perfected assignment of rents here, those rents are not included in the bankruptcy estate. Accordingly, we **reverse** the order of the bankruptcy court.

H. PREPETITION WAIVER OF STAY

CHAPTER 6

EXECUTORY CONTRACTS AND LEASES

A. EXECUTORY CONTRACTS

1. INTRODUCTION

2. DECISION TO ASSUME OR REJECT

3. MEANING OF "EXECUTORY CONTRACT"

4. REJECTION OF LICENSES OF INTELLECTUAL PROPERTY

> Add before the Problems following *Lubrizol* at p. 225:

A lingering issue in connection with §365(n) was whether a licensee of rights that fell outside of the definition of "intellectual property" also would be able to retain those rights in the event the debtor rejected the license, or whether the licensees of such rights would not be protected. After a circuit split emerged with respect to the most important of these omitted rights, trademarks, the Supreme Court took certiorari and handed down the decision that follows:

Mission Product Holdings, Inc. v. Tempnology, LLC

Supreme Court of the United States, 2019.
2019 U.S. LEXIS 3544.

KAGAN, J., delivered the opinion of the Court.

Section 365 of the Bankruptcy Code enables a debtor to "reject any executory contract"—meaning a contract that neither party has finished performing. The section further provides that a debtor's rejection of a contract under that authority "constitutes a breach of such contract." §365(g).

Today we consider the meaning of those provisions in the context of a trademark licensing agreement. The question is whether the debtor-licensor's rejection of that contract deprives the licensee of its rights to use the trademark. We hold it does not. A rejection breaches a contract but does not rescind it. And that means all the rights that would ordinarily survive a contract breach, including those conveyed here, remain in place.

I

This case arises from a licensing agreement gone wrong. Respondent Tempnology, LLC, manufactured clothing and accessories designed to stay

27

cool when used in exercise. It marketed those products under the brand name "Coolcore," using trademarks (*e.g.,* logos and labels) to distinguish the gear from other athletic apparel. In 2012, Tempnology entered into a contract with petitioner Mission Product Holdings, Inc. The agreement gave Mission an exclusive license to distribute certain Coolcore products in the United States. And more important here, it granted Mission a non-exclusive license to use the Coolcore trademarks, both in the United States and around the world. The agreement was set to expire in July 2016. But in September 2015, Tempnology filed a petition for Chapter 11 bankruptcy. And it soon afterward asked the Bankruptcy Court to allow it to "reject" the licensing agreement. §365(a).

... Section 365(a) of the Code provides that a "trustee [or debtor], subject to the court's approval, may assume or reject any executory contract." §365(a). A contract is executory if "performance remains due to some extent on both sides." *NLRB v. Bildisco & Bildisco*, 465 U. S. 513, 522, n. 6 (1984) (internal quotation marks omitted). ...

According to Section 365(g), "the rejection of an executory contract[ ] constitutes a breach of such contract." As both parties here agree, the counterparty thus has a claim against the estate for damages resulting from the debtor's nonperformance. But such a claim is unlikely to ever be paid in full. That is because the debtor's breach is deemed to occur "immediately before the date of the filing of the [bankruptcy] petition," rather than on the actual postpetition rejection date. §365(g)(1). By thus giving the counterparty a pre-petition claim, Section 365(g) places that party in the same boat as the debtor's unsecured creditors, who in a typical bankruptcy may receive only cents on the dollar. ...

In this case, the Bankruptcy Court (per usual) approved Tempnology's proposed rejection of its executory licensing agreement with Mission. That meant, as laid out above, two things on which the parties agree. First, Tempnology could stop performing under the contract. And second, Mission could assert (for whatever it might be worth) a pre-petition claim in the bankruptcy proceeding for damages resulting from Tempnology's nonperformance.

But Tempnology thought still another consequence ensued, and it returned to the Bankruptcy Court for a declaratory judgment confirming its view. According to Tempnology, its rejection of the contract also terminated the rights it had granted Mission to use the Coolcore trademarks. Tempnology based its argument on a negative inference. Several provisions in Section 365 state that a counterparty to specific kinds of agreements may keep exercising contractual rights after a debtor's rejection. For example, Section 365(h) provides that if a bankrupt landlord rejects a lease, the tenant need not move out; instead, she may stay and pay rent (just as she did before) until the lease term expires. And still closer to home, Section 365(n) sets out a similar rule for some types of intellectual property licenses: If the debtor-licensor rejects the agreement, the licensee can continue to use the property (typically, a patent), so long as it makes whatever payments the contract demands. But Tempnology pointed out that neither Section 365(n) nor any similar provision covers trademark licenses. So, it reasoned, in that sort of contract a different rule must apply: The debtor's rejection must extinguish the rights that the agreement had conferred on the trademark licensee. The Bankruptcy Court agreed. It held, relying on the same "negative inference," that Tempnology's rejection of the licensing agreement revoked Mission's right to use the Coolcore marks.

The Bankruptcy Appellate Panel reversed, relying heavily on a decision of the Court of Appeals for the Seventh Circuit about the effects of rejection on trademark licensing agreements. See *In re Tempnology, LLC*, 559 B. R. 809,

820–823 (Bkrtcy. App. Panel CA1 2016); *Sunbeam Products, Inc. v. Chicago Am. Mfg., LLC*, 686 F. 3d 372, 376–377 (CA7 2012). Rather than reason backward from Section 365(n) or similar provisions, the Panel focused on Section 365(g)'s statement that rejection of a contract "constitutes a breach." Outside bankruptcy, the court explained, the breach of an agreement does not eliminate rights the contract had already conferred on the non-breaching party. So neither could a rejection of an agreement in bankruptcy have that effect. A rejection "convert[s]" a "debtor's unfulfilled obligations" to a pre-petition damages claim. *Id.,* at 822 (quoting *Sunbeam*, 686 F. 3d, at 377). But it does not "terminate the contract" or "vaporize[ ]" the counterparty's rights. 559 B. R., at 820, 822 (quoting *Sunbeam*, 686 F. 3d, at 377). Mission could thus continue to use the Coolcore trademarks.

But the Court of Appeals for the First Circuit rejected the Panel's and Seventh Circuit's view, and reinstated the Bankruptcy Court decision terminating Mission's license. See *In re Tempnology, LLC*, 879 F. 3d 389 (2018). The majority first endorsed that court's inference from Section 365(n) and similar provisions. It next reasoned that special features of trademark law counsel against allowing a licensee to retain rights to a mark after the licensing agreement's rejection. Under that body of law, the majority stated, the trademark owner's "[f]ailure to monitor and exercise [quality] control" over goods associated with a trademark "jeopardiz[es] the continued validity of [its] own trademark rights." *Id.,* at 402. So if (the majority continued) a licensee can keep using a mark after an agreement's rejection, the licensor will need to carry on its monitoring activities. And according to the majority, that would frustrate "Congress's principal aim in providing for rejection": to "release the debtor's estate from burdensome obligations." *Ibid.* (internal quotation marks omitted). Judge Torruella dissented, mainly for the Seventh Circuit's reasons. See *id.,* at 405–407.

We granted certiorari to resolve the division between the First and Seventh Circuits. We now affirm the Seventh's reasoning and reverse the decision below.[1]

II

[The Court rejected Tempnology's claim that the case was moot]

III

What is the effect of a debtor's (or trustee's) rejection of a contract under Section 365 of the Bankruptcy Code? The parties and courts of appeals have offered us two starkly different answers. According to one view, a rejection has the same consequence as a contract breach outside bankruptcy: It gives the counterparty a claim for damages, while leaving intact the rights the counterparty has received under the contract. According to the other view, a rejection (except in a few spheres) has more the effect of a contract rescission in the non-bankruptcy world: Though also allowing a damages claim, the rejection terminates the whole agreement along with all rights it conferred. Today, we hold

---

[1] In its briefing before this Court, Mission contends that its exclusive distribution rights survived the licensing agreement's rejection for the same reason as its trademark rights did. But the First Circuit held that Mission had waived that argument, and we have no reason to doubt that conclusion. Our decision thus affects only Mission's trademark rights.

that both Section 365's text and fundamental principles of bankruptcy law command the first, rejection-as-breach approach. We reject the competing claim that by specifically enabling the counterparties in some contracts to retain rights after rejection, Congress showed that it wanted the counterparties in all other contracts to lose their rights. And we reject an argument for the rescission approach turning on the distinctive features of trademark licenses. Rejection of a contract— any contract—in bankruptcy operates not as a rescission but as a breach.

A

We start with the text of the Code's principal provisions on rejection—and find that it does much of the work. As noted earlier, Section 365(a) gives a debtor the option, subject to court approval, to "assume or reject any executory contract." And Section 365(g) describes what rejection means. Rejection "constitutes a breach of [an executory] contract," deemed to occur "immediately before the date of the filing of the petition." Or said more pithily for current purposes, a rejection is a breach. And "breach" is neither a defined nor a specialized bankruptcy term. It means in the Code what it means in contract law outside bankruptcy. See *Field v. Mans*, 516 U. S. 59, 69 (1995) (Congress generally meant for the Bankruptcy Code to "incorporate the established meaning" of "terms that have accumulated settled meaning" (internal quotation marks omitted)). So the first place to go in divining the effects of rejection is to nonbankruptcy contract law, which can tell us the effects of breach.

Consider a made-up executory contract to see how the law of breach works outside bankruptcy. A dealer leases a photocopier to a law firm, while agreeing to service it every month; in exchange, the firm commits to pay a monthly fee. During the lease term, the dealer decides to stop servicing the machine, thus breaching the agreement in a material way. The law firm now has a choice (assuming no special contract term or state law). The firm can keep up its side of the bargain, continuing to pay for use of the copier, while suing the dealer for damages from the service breach. Or the firm can call the whole deal off, halting its own payments and returning the copier, while suing for any damages incurred. See 13 R. Lord, Williston on Contracts §39:32, pp. 701–702 (4th ed. 2013) ("[W]hen a contract is breached in the course of performance, the injured party may elect to continue the contract or refuse to perform further"). But to repeat: The choice to terminate the agreement and send back the copier is for the *law firm*. By contrast, the *dealer* has no ability, based on its own breach, to terminate the agreement. Or otherwise said, the dealer cannot get back the copier just by refusing to show up for a service appointment. The contract gave the law firm continuing rights in the copier, which the dealer cannot unilaterally revoke.

And now to return to bankruptcy: If the rejection of the photocopier contract "constitutes a breach," as the Code says, then the same results should follow (save for one twist as to timing). Assume here that the dealer files a Chapter 11 petition and decides to reject its agreement with the law firm. That means, as above, that the dealer will stop servicing the copier. It means, too, that the law firm has an option about how to respond—continue the contract or walk away, while suing for whatever damages go with its choice. (Here is where the twist comes in: Because the rejection is deemed to occur "immediately before" bankruptcy, the firm's damages suit is treated as a pre-petition claim on the estate, which will likely receive only cents on the dollar.) And most important, it means that assuming the law firm wants to keep using the copier, the dealer cannot take it back. A rejection does not terminate the contract. When it occurs, the debtor and counterparty do not go back to their precontract positions. Instead, the counterparty retains the rights it has received under the agreement. As after a breach, so too after a rejection, those rights survive.

All of this, it will hardly surprise you to learn, is not just about photocopier leases. Sections 365(a) and (g) speak broadly, to "any executory contract[s]." Many licensing agreements involving trademarks or other property are of that kind (including, all agree, the Tempnology-Mission contract). The licensor not only grants a license, but provides associated goods or services during its term; the licensee pays continuing royalties or fees. If the licensor breaches the agreement outside bankruptcy (again, barring any special contract term or state law), everything said above goes. In particular, the breach does not revoke the license or stop the licensee from doing what it allows. See, *e.g., Sunbeam*, 686 F. 3d, at 376 ("Outside of bankruptcy, a licensor's breach does not terminate a licensee's right to use [the licensed] intellectual property"). And because rejection "constitutes a breach," §365(g), the same consequences follow in bankruptcy. The debtor can stop performing its remaining obligations under the agreement. But the debtor cannot rescind the license already conveyed. So the licensee can continue to do whatever the license authorizes.

In preserving those rights, Section 365 reflects a general bankruptcy rule: The estate cannot possess anything more than the debtor itself did outside bankruptcy. See *Board of Trade of Chicago v. Johnson*, 264 U. S. 1, 15 (1924) (establishing that principle); §541(a)(1) (defining the estate to include the "interests *of the debtor* in property" (emphasis added)). As one bankruptcy scholar has put the point: Whatever "limitation[s] on the debtor's property [apply] outside of bankruptcy[ ] appl[y] inside of bankruptcy as well. A debtor's property does not shrink by happenstance of bankruptcy, but it does not expand, either." D. Baird, Elements of Bankruptcy 97 (6th ed. 2014). So if the not-yet debtor was subject to a counterparty's contractual right (say, to retain a copier or use a trademark), so too is the trustee or debtor once the bankruptcy petition has been filed. The rejection-as-breach rule (but *not* the rejection-as-rescission rule) ensures that result. By insisting that the same counterparty rights survive rejection as survive breach, the rule prevents a debtor in bankruptcy from recapturing interests it had given up.

And conversely, the rejection-as-rescission approach would circumvent the Code's stringent limits on "avoidance" actions—the exceptional cases in which trustees (or debtors) may indeed unwind pre-bankruptcy transfers that undermine the bankruptcy process. The most notable example is for fraudulent conveyances—usually, something-for-nothing transfers that deplete the estate (and so cheat creditors) on the eve of bankruptcy. See §548(a). A trustee's avoidance powers are laid out in a discrete set of sections in the Code, see §§544–553, far away from Section 365. And they can be invoked in only narrow circumstances—unlike the power of rejection, which may be exercised for any plausible economic reason. See, *e.g.,* §548(a) (describing the requirements for avoiding fraudulent transfers). If trustees (or debtors) could use rejection to rescind previously granted interests, then rejection would become functionally equivalent to avoidance. Both, that is, would roll back a prior transfer. And that result would subvert everything the Code does to keep avoidances cabined—so they do not threaten the rule that the estate can take only what the debtor possessed before filing. Again, then, core tenets of bankruptcy law push in the same direction as Section 365's text: Rejection is breach, and has only its consequences.

B

Tempnology's main argument to the contrary, here as in the courts below, rests on a negative inference. Several provisions of Section 365, Tempnology notes, "identif[y] categories of contracts under which a counterparty" may retain specified contract rights "notwithstanding rejection." Sections 365(h) and (i) make clear that certain purchasers and lessees of real property and timeshare interests can continue to exercise rights after a debtor has rejected the lease or sales contract. See §365(h)(1) (real-property leases); §365(i) (real-property sales contracts); §§365(h)(2), (i) (timeshare interests). And Section 365(n) similarly provides that licensees of some intellectual property—but not trademarks—retain contractual rights after rejection. See §365(n); §101(35A). Tempnology argues from those provisions that the ordinary consequence of rejection must be something different—*i.e.,* the termination, rather than survival, of contractual rights previously granted. Otherwise, Tempnology concludes, the statute's "general rule" would "swallow the exceptions."

But that argument pays too little heed to the main provisions governing rejection and too much to subsidiary ones. On the one hand, it offers no account of how to read Section 365(g) (recall, rejection "constitutes a breach") to say essentially its opposite (*i.e.,* that rejection and breach have divergent consequences). On the other hand, it treats as a neat, reticulated scheme of "narrowly tailored exception[s]," *id.,* at 36 (emphasis deleted), what history reveals to be anything but. Each of the provisions Tempnology highlights emerged at a different time, over a span of half a century. See, *e.g.,* 52 Stat. 881 (1938) (real property leases); §1(b), 102 Stat. 2538 (1988) (intellectual property). And each responded to a discrete problem—as often as not, correcting a judicial ruling of just the kind Tempnology urges. See Andrew, Executive Contracts in Bankruptcy, 59 U. Colo. L. Rev. 845, 911–912, 916–919 (1988) (identifying judicial decisions that the provisions overturned); compare, *e.g., In re Sombrero Reef Club, Inc.,* 18 B. R. 612, 618–619 (Bkrtcy. Ct. SD Fla. 1982), with, *e.g.,* §§365(h)(2), (i). Read as generously as possible to Tempnology, this mash-up of legislative interventions says nothing much of anything about the content of Section 365(g)'s general rule. Read less generously, it affirmatively refutes Tempnology's rendition. As one bankruptcy scholar noted after an exhaustive review of the history: "What the legislative record [reflects] is that whenever Congress has been confronted with the consequences of the [view that rejection terminates all contractual rights], it has expressed its disapproval." Andrew, 59 U. Colo. L. Rev., at 928. On that account, Congress enacted the provisions, as and when needed, to reinforce or clarify the general rule that contractual rights survive rejection.[2]

Consider more closely, for example, Congress's enactment of Section 365(n), which addresses certain intellectual property licensing agreements. No

---

[2] At the same time, Congress took the opportunity when drafting those provisions to fill in certain details, generally left to state law, about the post-rejection relationship between the debtor and counter- party. See, *e.g.,* Andrew, Executory Contracts in Bankruptcy, 59 U. Colo. L. Rev. 845, 903, n. 200 (1988) (describing Congress's addition of subsidiary rules for real property leases in Section 365(h)); Brief for United States as *Amicus Curiae* 29 (noting that Congress similarly set out detailed rules for patent licenses in Section 365(n)). The provisions are therefore not redundant of Section 365(g): Each sets out a remedial scheme embellishing on or tweaking the general rejection-as-breach rule.

one disputes how that provision came about. In *Lubrizol Enterprises v. Richmond Metal Finishers,* the Fourth Circuit held that a debtor's rejection of an executory contract worked to revoke its grant of a patent license. See 756 F. 2d 1043, 1045–1048 (1985). In other words, *Lubrizol* adopted the same rule for patent licenses that the First Circuit announced for trademark licenses here. Congress sprang into action, drafting Section 365(n) to reverse *Lubrizol* and ensure the continuation of patent (and some other intellectual property) licensees' rights. See 102 Stat. 2538 (1988); S. Rep. No. 100–505, pp. 2–4 (1988) (explaining that Section 365(n) "corrects [*Lubrizol's*] perception" that "Section 365 was ever intended to be a mechanism for stripping innocent licensee[s] of rights"). As Tempnology highlights, that provision does not cover trademark licensing agreements, which continue to fall, along with most other contracts, within Section 365(g)'s general rule. But what of that? Even put aside the claim that Section 365(n) is part of a pattern—that Congress whacked Tempnology's view of rejection wherever it raised its head. See *supra,* at 13. Still, Congress's repudiation of *Lubrizol* for patent contracts does not show any intent to *ratify* that decision's approach for almost all others. Which is to say that no negative inference arises. Congress did nothing in adding Section 365(n) to alter the natural reading of Section 365(g)—that rejection and breach have the same results.

Tempnology's remaining argument turns on the way special features of trademark law may affect the fulfillment of the Code's goals. Like the First Circuit below, Tempnology here focuses on a trademark licensor's duty to monitor and "exercise quality control over the goods and services sold" under a license. Absent those efforts to keep up quality, the mark will naturally decline in value and may eventually become altogether invalid. See 3 J. McCarthy, Trademarks and Unfair Competition §18:48, pp. 18–129, 18–133 (5th ed. 2018). So (Tempnology argues) unless rejection of a trademark licensing agreement terminates the licensee's rights to use the mark, the debtor will have to choose between expending scarce resources on quality control and risking the loss of a valuable asset. "Either choice," Tempnology concludes, "would impede a [debtor's] ability to reorganize," thus "undermining a fundamental purpose of the Code."

To begin with, that argument is a mismatch with Tempnology's reading of Section 365. The argument is trademark-specific. But Tempnology's reading of Section 365 is not. Remember, Tempnology construes that section to mean that a debtor's rejection of a contract terminates the counterparty's rights "unless the contract falls within an express statutory exception." That construction treats trademark agreements identically to most other contracts; the only agreements getting different treatment are those falling within the discrete provisions just discussed. And indeed, Tempnology could not have discovered, however hard it looked, any trademark-specific rule in Section 365. That section's special provisions, as all agree, do not mention trademarks; and the general provisions speak, well, generally. So Tempnology is essentially arguing that distinctive features of trademarks should persuade us to adopt a construction of Section 365 that will govern not just trademark agreements, but pretty nearly every executory contract. However serious Tempnology's trademark-related concerns, that would allow the tail to wag the Doberman.

And even putting aside that incongruity, Tempnology's plea to facilitate trademark licensors' reorganizations cannot overcome what Sections 365(a) and (g) direct. The Code of course aims to make reorganizations possible. But it does not permit anything and everything that might advance that goal. See, *e.g., Florida Dept. of Revenue v. Piccadilly Cafeterias, Inc.,* 554 U. S. 33, 51

(2008) (observing that in enacting Chapter 11, Congress did not have "a single purpose," but "str[uck] a balance" among multiple competing interests (internal quotation marks omitted)). Here, Section 365 provides a debtor like Tempnology with a powerful tool: Through rejection, the debtor can escape all of its future contract obligations, without having to pay much of anything in return. But in allowing rejection of those contractual duties, Section 365 does not grant the debtor an exemption from all the burdens that generally applicable law—whether involving contracts or trademarks—imposes on property owners. See 28 U. S. C. §959(b) (requiring a trustee to manage the estate in accordance with applicable law). Nor does Section 365 relieve the debtor of the need, against the backdrop of that law, to make economic decisions about preserving the estate's value—such as whether to invest the resources needed to maintain a trademark. In thus delineating the burdens that a debtor may and may not escape, Congress also weighed (among other things) the legitimate interests and expectations of the debtor's counterparties. The resulting balance may indeed impede some reorganizations, of trademark licensors and others. But that is only to say that Section 365's edict that rejection is breach expresses a more complex set of aims than Tempnology acknowledges.

IV

For the reasons stated above, we hold that under Section 365, a debtor's rejection of an executory contract in bankruptcy has the same effect as a breach outside bankruptcy. Such an act cannot rescind rights that the contract previously granted. Here, that construction of Section 365 means that the debtor-licensor's rejection cannot revoke the trademark license.

We accordingly reverse the judgment of the Court of Appeals and remand the case for further proceedings consistent with this opinion.

It is so ordered.

[The concurring opinion of Justice Sotomayor and the dissenting opinion of Justice Gorsuch are omitted.]

> On p. 225, delete the current text of Problem 1 and add a new Note before the Problems:

In her concurring opinion in *Tempnology*, Justice Sotomayor points out that §365(n) "alters the general rejection rule in several respects. For example, a covered licensee that chooses to retain its rights postrejection must make all of its royalty payments; the licensee has no right to deduct damages from its payments even if it otherwise could have done so under nonbankruptcy law. §365(n)(2)(C)(i)." Because trademark licenses are governed by the general rules that apply outside of bankruptcy (including the right of the trademark licensee to deduct damages from its payments after a breach), rather than by §365(n), the treatment of rejected trademark licenses will differ in some respects from the treatment of rejected intellectual property licenses that are covered by §365(n).

5. CONTRACTS NOT ASSIGNABLE UNDER NONBANKRUPTCY LAW

6. ENFORCEMENT BEFORE ASSUMPTION OR REJECTION

B. LEASES

1. REJECTION BY DIP AS LESSOR

> Add to Note 3 following *Qualitech Steel* at pp. 258-59:

The Ninth Circuit recently added further fuel to the *Qualitech Steel* fire by following the decision in *Matter of Spanish Peaks Holdings II, LLC*, 872 F.3d 892 (9th Cir. 2017).

2. REJECTION BY DIP AS LESSEE

3. LIABILITY FOR USE OF LEASED PROPERTY

4. EVICTING THE DIP

5. ASSUMPTION AND ASSIGNMENT

CHAPTER 7

THE AVOIDING POWERS

A. PREFERENCES

1. THE CONCEPT OF A PREFERENCE

2. TRANSFER OF DEBTOR'S INTEREST IN PROPERTY AND THE "EARMARKING" DOCTRINE

3. THE PREFERENCE PERIOD

4. CONTEMPORANEOUS EXCHANGES

5. FALSE PREFERENCES: DELAYED PERFECTION OF LIENS

6. ORDINARY COURSE PAYMENTS

7. THE "SUBSEQUENT ADVANCE" RULE

8. SECURITY INTERESTS IN INVENTORY AND ACCOUNTS RECEIVABLE

9. OTHER PROTECTED TRANSFERS

10. INSIDER PREFERENCES

Insert before Problem at p. 314:

The Ninth Circuit recently added yet another relevant wrinkle, holding in the Chapter 11 context that a person or entity that purchases a claim from an insider is not itself an insider if the purchaser would not otherwise qualify. *In re Village at Lakeridge, LLC.*, 814 F.3d 993 (9th Cir. 2016). The Supreme Court granted *certiorari* in *Lakeridge* for the very limited purpose of addressing the appropriate standard of appellate review of a bankruptcy court determination of non-statutory insider status, ultimately holding that review of bankruptcy court determinations of non-statutory insider status is deferential under the "clearly erroneous" standard. *US Bank, NA v. Village of Lakeridge*, 138 S.Ct. 960 (2018). Four concurring Justices led by Justice Sotomayor, however, went on to question the Ninth Circuit's existing legal standard for determining non-statutory insider status. The Ninth Circuit's two-prong test directs courts to consider whether (i) the putative insider has a relationship comparable to those persons in the enumerated statutory categories and (ii) the transaction is at arms-length. *Statutory* insiders incur the liability associated with their insider status regardless of whether they otherwise deal at arms-length with the debtor. The concurring Justices therefore doubted whether the second prong of this test, which focuses on the transaction rather than the relationship between the debtor and the counterparty, was appropriate in the case of *non-statutory* insiders.

11. Letters of Credit

B. Setoff

C. Fraudulent Transfers

1. Actual Fraud

2. Constructive Fraud

3. Foreclosures

> Insert following Note 3, p. 341:

In *In re Tracht Gut, LLC*, 836 F.3d 1146, 1153 (9th Cir. 2016), the Ninth Circuit held that the logic of *BFP* applies to California tax sales, given similarities to the foreclosure sale at issue in *BFP*. *Contra In re GGI Properties LLC*, 568 B.R. 231 (Bankr. D.N.J.2017) (New Jersey tax sale); *see also In re Hackler*, 571 B.R. 662 (Bankr. D.N.J. 2017), *aff'd*, 588 B.R. 394 (D.N.J. 2018) (*BFP* not applicable in preference attack on tax sale).

4. Ponzi Schemes

> Insert before Problem, p. 343:

In an influential and striking series of rulings in the *Madoff* cases, the courts in the Southern District of New York and the Second Circuit have set up substantial barriers to the recovery of pre-bankruptcy transfers made to investors. Most importantly, by broadly construing the scope of the settlement payments defense of §546(e) to include transfers out of the fraudulent Madoff funds as securities transactions (even though the Madoff funds never actually held or traded any securities) the courts have limited disgorgement actions to claims for actual fraud under §548(a)(1)(A). This gives defendants the benefit of the short two-year federal statute of limitations. The courts also have given broad construction to the statutory "good faith" defense protecting even sophisticated investors who did not have actual knowledge of the fraud even though they had ample reason to know or investigate. The most recent *Madoff* decision halted this trend in one respect, however. After the lower court ruled that foreign investors, and even U.S, based investors who invested through offshore "feeder funds," were insulated from disgorgement because of jurisdictional limitations, the Second Circuit reversed in *In re Picard*, 917 F.3d 85 (2d. Cir. 2019). The Second Circuit held that the focus is on the debtor's initial transfer, not the location of the transferee, and that neither the presumption against extraterritoriality nor international comity principles preclude recovery from foreign subsequent transferees.

| Insert at the end of Problem, p. 343: |

In *In re Provident Royalties, LLC*, 581 B.R. 185 (Bankr. N.D. Tex. 2017), the court wrestled with the question how to apply the "single satisfaction" rule in §550(d) to a subsequent transferee where the initial transferee, which had transferred some but not all of a group of transfers to the subsequent transferee, settled its liability for significantly less than the full amount. The court concluded that crediting the settlement proceeds solely against transfers that were not retransferred to the subsequent transferee would be too favorable to the trustee. On the other hand, allocating the settlement entirely to transfers that were retransferred to the subsequent transferee would unduly benefit the subsequent transferee by reducing its liability to the trustee by the full amount of the settlement recovered from the initial transferee. Instead, the court independently allocated the settlement among the transfers. The amounts the court attributed to transfers that were in turn retransferred to the subsequent transferee reduced the subsequent transferee's liability for those transfers.

5A. SETTLEMENT PAYMENTS DEFENSE

| Insert on p. 345, immediately prior to current Section 5, this new Section 5A: |

The special defense for settlement and margin payments, which is briefly described in the TENTH EDITION note 3 on p. 344, has become a major factor in many substantial bankruptcy cases. Originally enacted in 1982, §546(e) was designed to protect stockbrokers and commodities brokers who received payments in connection with their normal securities trading activities in public markets from being forced to disgorge the payments if the payments might otherwise technically qualify as preferences or fraudulent conveyances.

Although the safe harbor was intended to address a relatively narrow concern, read broadly, it seems to insulate any payment made by or to a financial institution, even if the financial institution is merely passing the payment on to its real recipient and does not implicate trading in public securities markets. Because financial institutions serve as intermediaries in virtually all transactions of any significance, the safe harbor read broadly can make it very difficult for the Trustee to avoid even obviously preferential or fraudulent transfers.

The question of the proper scope of §546(e) involves very high stakes and the issue divided the circuit courts. The Supreme Court finally addressed the question of whether otherwise avoidable transactions effectuated through financial intermediaries were within the safe harbor in this case:

Merit Management Group LP v. FTI Consulting, Inc.

Supreme Court of the United States, 2018.
138 S.Ct. 883.

Justice SOTOMAYOR delivered the opinion of the Court:

To maximize the funds available for, and ensure equity in, the distribution to creditors in a bankruptcy proceeding, the Bankruptcy Code gives a trustee the power to invalidate a limited category of transfers by the debtor or transfers of an interest of the debtor in property. Those powers, referred to as "avoiding powers," are not without limits, however, as the Code sets out a number of exceptions. The operation of one such exception, the securities safe harbor, 11 U.S.C. §546(e), is at issue in this case. Specifically, this Court is asked to determine how the safe harbor operates in the context of a transfer that was executed via one or more transactions, e.g., a transfer from A → D that was executed via B and C as intermediaries, such that the component parts of the transfer include A → B → C → D. If a trustee seeks to avoid the A → D transfer, and the §546(e) safe harbor is invoked as a defense, the question becomes:

When determining whether the §546(e) securities safe harbor saves the transfer from avoidance, should courts look to the transfer that the trustee seeks to avoid (i.e., A → D) to determine whether that transfer meets the safe-harbor criteria, or should courts look also to any component parts of the overarching transfer (i.e., A → B → C → D)?

The Court concludes that the plain meaning of §546(e) dictates that the only relevant transfer for purposes of the safe harbor is the transfer that the trustee seeks to avoid.

I

A

Because the §546(e) safe harbor operates as a limit to the general avoiding powers of a bankruptcy trustee,1 we begin with a review of those powers. Chapter 5 of the Bankruptcy Code affords bankruptcy trustees the authority to "se[t] aside certain types of transfers ... and ... recaptur[e] the value of those avoided transfers for the benefit of the estate." Tabb §6.2, p. 474. These avoiding powers "help implement the core principles of bankruptcy." Id., §6.1, at 468. For example, some "deter the race of diligence of creditors to dismember the debtor before bankruptcy" and promote "equality of distribution." *Union Bank v. Wolas* (1991); see also Tabb §6.2. Others set aside transfers that "unfairly or improperly deplete ... assets or ... dilute the claims against those assets." 5 Collier on Bankruptcy ¶ 548.01, p. 548–10 (16th ed. 2017); see also Tabb §6.2, at 475 (noting that some avoiding powers are designed "to ensure that the debtor deals fairly with its creditors").

Sections 544 through 553 of the Code outline the circumstances under which a trustee may pursue avoidance. See, e.g., 11 U.S.C. §544(a) (setting out circumstances under which a trustee can avoid unrecorded liens and conveyances); §544(b) (detailing power to avoid based on rights that unsecured creditors have under nonbankruptcy law); §545 (setting out criteria that allow a trustee to avoid a statutory lien); §547 (detailing criteria for avoidance of so-called "preferential transfers"). The particular avoidance provision at issue here is §548(a), which provides that a "trustee may avoid" certain fraudulent transfers "of an interest of the debtor in property." §548(a)(1). Section 548(a)(1)(A) addresses so-called "actually" fraudulent transfers, which are "made ... with actual intent to hinder, delay, or defraud any entity to which the debtor was or became … indebted." Section 548(a)(1)(B) addresses "constructively" fraudulent transfers. *See BFP v. Resolution Trust Corporation* (1994). As relevant to this case, the statute defines constructive fraud in part as when a debtor:

"(B)(i) received less than a reasonably equivalent value in exchange for such transfer or obligation; and

"(ii)(I) was insolvent on the date that such transfer was made or such obligation was incurred, or became insolvent as a result of such transfer or obligation. 11 U.S.C. §548(a)(1).

If a transfer is avoided, §550 identifies the parties from whom the trustee may recover either the transferred property or the value of that property to return to the bankruptcy estate. Section 550(a) provides, in relevant part, that "to the extent that a transfer is avoided … the trustee may recover … the property transferred, or, if the court so orders, the value of such property" from "the initial transferee of such transfer or the entity for whose benefit such transfer was made," or from "any immediate or mediate transferee of such initial transferee." §550(a).

B

The Code sets out a number of limits on the exercise of these avoiding powers. See, e.g., §546(a) (setting statute of limitations for avoidance actions); §§546(c)-(d) (setting certain policy-based exceptions to avoiding powers); §548(a)(2) (setting limit to avoidance of "a charitable contribution to a qualified religious or charitable entity or organization"). Central to this case is the securities safe harbor set forth in §546(e), which provides (as presently codified and in full):

"Notwithstanding sections 544, 545, 547, 548(a)(1)(B), and 548(b) of this title, the trustee may not avoid a transfer that is a margin payment, as defined in section 101, 741, or 761 of this title, or settlement payment, as defined in section 101 or 741 of this title, made by or to (or for the benefit of) a commodity broker, forward contract merchant, stockbroker, financial institution, financial participant, or securities clearing agency, or that is a transfer made by or to (or for the benefit of) a commodity broker, forward contract merchant, stockbroker, financial institution, financial participant, or securities clearing agency, in connection with a securities contract, as defined in section 741(7), commodity contract, as defined in section 761(4), or forward contract, that is made before the commencement of the case, except under section 548(a)(1)(A) of this title."

The predecessor to this securities safe harbor, formerly codified at 11 U.S.C. §764(c), was enacted in 1978 against the backdrop of a district court decision in a case called *Seligson v. New York Produce Exchange*, 394 F.Supp. 125 (S.D.N.Y.1975), which involved a transfer by a bankrupt commodity broker. See S. Rep. No. 95–989, pp. 8, 106 (1978); see also Brubaker, *Understanding the Scope of the §546(e) Securities Safe Harbor Through the Concept of the "Transfer" Sought To Be Avoided*, 37 Bkrtcy. L. Letter 11–12 (July 2017). The bankruptcy trustee in *Seligson* filed suit seeking to avoid over $12 million in margin payments made by the commodity broker debtor to a clearing association on the basis that the transfer was constructively fraudulent. The clearing association attempted to defend on the theory that it was a mere "conduit" for the transmission of the margin payments. The District Court found, however, triable issues of fact on that question and denied summary judgment, leaving the clearing association exposed to the risk of significant liability. See id., at 135–136. Following that decision, Congress enacted the §764(c) safe harbor, providing that "the trustee may not avoid a transfer that is a margin payment to or deposit with a commodity broker or forward contract merchant or is a settlement payment made by a clearing organization." 92 Stat. 2619, codified at 11 U.S.C. §764(c) (repealed 1982).

Congress amended the securities safe harbor exception over the years, each time expanding the categories of covered transfers or entities. In 1982, Congress expanded the safe harbor to protect margin and settlement payments "made by or to a commodity broker, forward contract merchant, stockbroker, or securities clearing agency." §4, 96 Stat. 236, codified at 11 U.S.C. §546(d). Two years later Congress added "financial institution" to the list of protected entities. See §461(d), 98 Stat. 377, codified at 11 U.S.C. §546(e).[2] In 2005, Congress again expanded the list of protected entities to include a "financial participant" (defined as an entity conducting certain high-value transactions). See §907(b), 119 Stat. 181–182; 11 U.S.C. §101(22A). And, in 2006, Congress amended the provision to cover transfers made in connection with securities contracts, commodity contracts, and forward contracts. §5(b)(1), 120 Stat. 2697–2698. The 2006 amendment also modified the statute to its current form by adding the new parenthetical phrase "(or for the benefit of)" after "by or to," so that the safe harbor now covers transfers made "by or to (or for the benefit of)" one of the covered entities. Id., at 2697.

C

With this background, we now turn to the facts of this case, which comes to this Court from the world of competitive harness racing (a form of horse racing). Harness racing is a closely regulated industry in Pennsylvania, and the Commonwealth requires a license to operate a racetrack. The number of available licenses is limited, and in 2003 two companies, Valley View Downs, LP, and Bedford Downs Management Corporation, were in competition for the last harness-racing license in Pennsylvania.

Valley View and Bedford Downs needed the harness-racing license to open a "racino," which is a clever moniker for racetrack casino, "a racing facility with slot machines." Brief for Petitioner 8. Both companies were stopped before the finish line, because in 2005 the Pennsylvania State Harness Racing

---

[2] The term "financial institution" is defined as:

"(A) a Federal reserve bank, or an entity that is a commercial or savings bank, industrial savings bank, savings and loan association, trust company, federally-insured credit union, or receiver, liquidating agent, or conservator for such entity and, when any such Federal reserve bank, receiver, liquidating agent, conservator or entity is acting as agent or custodian for a customer (whether or not a 'customer', as defined in section 741) in connection with a securities contract (as defined in section 741) such customer; or

"(B) in connection with a securities contract (as defined in section 741) an investment company registered under the Investment Company Act of 1940." 11 U.S.C. §101(22).

The parties here do not contend that either the debtor or petitioner in this case qualified as a "financial institution" by virtue of its status as a "customer" under §101(22)(A). Petitioner Merit Management Group, LP, discussed this definition only in footnotes and did not argue that it somehow dictates the outcome in this case. See Brief for Petitioner 45, n. 14; Reply Brief 14, n. 6. We therefore do not address what impact, if any, §101(22)(A) would have in the application of the §546(e) safe harbor.

CHAPTER. 7—THE AVOIDING POWERS

Commission denied both applications. The Pennsylvania Supreme Court up-
held those denials in 2007, but allowed the companies to reapply for the license.

Instead of continuing to compete for the last available harness-racing license, Valley View and Bedford Downs entered into an agreement to resolve
their ongoing feud. Under that agreement, Bedford Downs withdrew as a com-
petitor for the harness-racing license, and Valley View was to purchase all of
Bedford Downs' stock for $55 million after Valley View obtained the license.

With Bedford Downs out of the race, the Pennsylvania Harness Racing
Commission awarded Valley View the last harness-racing license. Valley View
proceeded with the corporate acquisition required by the parties' agreement
and arranged for the Cayman Islands branch of Credit Suisse to finance the $55
million purchase price as part of a larger $850 million transaction. Credit Suisse
wired the $55 million to Citizens Bank of Pennsylvania, which had agreed to
serve as the third-party escrow agent for the transaction. The Bedford Downs
shareholders, including petitioner Merit Management Group, LP, deposited
their stock certificates into escrow as well. At closing, Valley View received
the Bedford Downs stock certificates, and in October 2007 Citizens Bank dis-
bursed $47.5 million to the Bedford Downs shareholders, with $7.5 million
remaining in escrow at Citizens Bank under the multiyear indemnification
holdback period provided for in the parties' agreement. Citizens Bank dis-
bursed that $7.5 million installment to the Bedford Downs shareholders in Oc-
tober 2010, after the holdback period ended. All told, Merit received approximately $16.5 million from the sale of its Bedford Downs stock to Valley View.
Notably, the closing statement for the transaction reflected Valley View as the
"Buyer," the Bedford Downs shareholders as the "Sellers," and $55 million as
the "Purchase Price."

In the end, Valley View never got to open its racino. Although it had secured the last harness-racing license, it was unable to secure a separate gaming
license for the operation of the slot machines in the time set out in its financing
package. Valley View and its parent company, Centaur, LLC, thereafter filed
for Chapter 11 bankruptcy. The Bankruptcy Court confirmed a reorganization
plan and appointed respondent FTI Consulting, Inc., to serve as trustee of the
Centaur litigation trust.

FTI filed suit against Merit in the Northern District of Illinois, seeking to
avoid the $16.5 million transfer from Valley View to Merit for the sale of Bed-
ford Downs' stock. The complaint alleged that the transfer was constructively
fraudulent under §548(a)(1)(B) of the Code because Valley View was insolvent
when it purchased Bedford Downs and "significantly overpaid" for the Bedford
Downs stock. Merit moved for judgment on the pleadings under Federal Rule
of Civil Procedure 12(c), contending that the §546(e) safe harbor barred FTI
from avoiding the Valley View–to–Merit transfer. According to Merit, the safe
harbor applied because the transfer was a "settlement payment … made by or
to (or for the benefit of)" a covered "financial institution"—here, Credit Suisse
and Citizens Bank.

The District Court granted the Rule 12(c) motion, reasoning that the
§546(e) safe harbor applied because the financial institutions transferred or received funds in connection with a "settlement payment" or "securities contract."[5] The Court of Appeals for the Seventh Circuit reversed, holding that the

---

[5] The parties do not ask this Court to determine whether the transaction at issue in
this case qualifies as a transfer that is a "settlement payment" or made in connection with

§546(e) safe harbor did not protect transfers in which financial institutions served as mere conduits. This Court granted certiorari to resolve a conflict among the circuit courts as to the proper application of the §546(e) safe harbor.[6]

II

The question before this Court is whether the transfer between Valley View and Merit implicates the safe harbor exception because the transfer was "made by or to (or for the benefit of) a ... financial institution." §546(e). The parties and the lower courts dedicate much of their attention to the definition of the words "by or to (or for the benefit of)" as used in §546(e), and to the question whether there is a requirement that the "financial institution" or other covered entity have a beneficial interest in or dominion and control over the transferred property in order to qualify for safe harbor protection. In our view, those inquiries put the proverbial cart before the horse. Before a court can determine whether a transfer was made by or to or for the benefit of a covered entity, the court must first identify the relevant transfer to test in that inquiry. At bottom, that is the issue the parties dispute in this case.

On one side, Merit posits that the Court should look not only to the Valley View–to–Merit end-to-end transfer, but also to all its component parts. Here, those component parts include one transaction by Credit Suisse to Citizens Bank (i.e., the transmission of the $16.5 million from Credit Suisse to escrow at Citizens Bank), and two transactions by Citizens Bank to Merit (i.e., the transmission of $16.5 million over two installments by Citizens Bank as escrow agent to Merit). Because those component parts include transactions by and to financial institutions, Merit contends that §546(e) bars avoidance.

FTI, by contrast, maintains that the only relevant transfer for purposes of the §546(e) safe-harbor inquiry is the overarching transfer between Valley View and Merit of $16.5 million for purchase of the stock, which is the transfer that the trustee seeks to avoid under §548(a)(1)(B). Because that transfer was not made by, to, or for the benefit of a financial institution, FTI contends that the safe harbor has no application.

The Court agrees with FTI. The language of §546(e), the specific context in which that language is used, and the broader statutory structure all support the conclusion that the relevant transfer for purposes of the §546(e) safe-harbor inquiry is the overarching transfer that the trustee seeks to avoid under one of the substantive avoidance provisions.

A

Our analysis begins with the text of §546(e), and we look to both "the language itself [and] the specific context in which that language is used ...." *Robinson v. Shell Oil Co.* (1997). The pertinent language provides:

---

a "securities contract" as those terms are used in §546(e), nor is that determination necessary for resolution of the question presented.

[6] Compare *In re Quebecor World (USA) Inc.,* 719 F.3d 94, 99 (C.A.2 2013) (finding the safe harbor applicable where covered entity was intermediary); *In re QSI Holdings, Inc.,* 571 F.3d 545, 551 (C.A.6 2009) (same); *Contemporary Indus. Corp. v. Frost,* 564 F.3d 981, 987 (C.A.8 2009) (same); *In re Resorts Int'l, Inc.,* 181 F.3d 505, 516 (C.A.3 1999) (same); *In re Kaiser Steel Corp.,* 952 F.2d 1230, 1240 (C.A.10 1991) (same), with *In re Munford, Inc.,* 98 F.3d 604, 610 (C.A.11 1996) (*per curiam*) (rejecting applicability of safe harbor where covered entity was intermediary).

"Notwithstanding sections 544, 545, 547, 548(a)(1)(B), and 548(b) of this title, the trustee may not avoid a transfer that is a … settlement payment … made by or to (or for the benefit of) a … financial institution … or that is a transfer made by or to (or for the benefit of) a … financial institution … in connection with a securities contract …, except under section 548(a)(1)(A) of this title."

The very first clause—"Notwithstanding sections 544, 545, 547, 548(a)(1)(B), and 548(b) of this title"—already begins to answer the question. It indicates that §546(e) operates as an exception to the avoiding powers afforded to the trustee under the substantive avoidance provisions. See A. SCALIA & B. GARNER, READING LAW: THE INTERPRETATION OF LEGAL TEXTS 126 (2012) ("A dependent phrase that begins with notwithstanding indicates that the main clause that it introduces or follows derogates from the provision to which it refers"). That is, when faced with a transfer that is otherwise avoidable, §546(e) provides a safe harbor notwithstanding that avoiding power. From the outset, therefore, the text makes clear that the starting point for the §546(e) inquiry is the substantive avoiding power under the provisions expressly listed in the "notwithstanding" clause and, consequently, the transfer that the trustee seeks to avoid as an exercise of those powers.

Then again in the very last clause—"except under section 548(a)(1)(A) of this title"—the text reminds us that the focus of the inquiry is the transfer that the trustee seeks to avoid. It does so by creating an exception to the exception, providing that "the trustee may not avoid a transfer" that meets the covered transaction and entity criteria of the safe harbor, "except" for an actually fraudulent transfer under §548(a)(1)(A). 11 U.S.C. §546(e). By referring back to a specific type of transfer that falls within the avoiding power, Congress signaled that the exception applies to the overarching transfer that the trustee seeks to avoid, not any component part of that transfer.

Reinforcing that reading of the safe-harbor provision, the section heading for §546—within which the securities safe harbor is found—is: "Limitations on avoiding powers." Although section headings cannot limit the plain meaning of a statutory text, *see Florida Dept. of Revenue v. Piccadilly Cafeterias, Inc.* (2008), "they supply cues" as to what Congress intended, *see Yates v. United States* (2015). In this case, the relevant section heading demonstrates the close connection between the transfer that the trustee seeks to avoid and the transfer that is exempted from that avoiding power pursuant to the safe harbor.

The rest of the statutory text confirms what the "notwithstanding" and "except" clauses and the section heading begin to suggest. The safe harbor provides that "the trustee may not avoid" certain transfers. §546(e). Naturally, that text invites scrutiny of the transfers that "the trustee may avoid," the parallel language used in the substantive avoiding powers provisions. See §544(a) (providing that "the trustee … may avoid" transfers falling under that provision); §545 (providing that "[t]he trustee may avoid" certain statutory liens); §547(b) (providing that "the trustee may avoid" certain preferential transfers); §548(a)(1) (providing that "[t]he trustee may avoid" certain fraudulent transfers). And if any doubt remained, the language that follows dispels that doubt: The transfer that the "the trustee may not avoid" is specified to be "a transfer that is" either a "settlement payment" or made "in connection with a securities contract." §546(e) (emphasis added). Not a transfer that involves. Not a transfer that comprises. But a transfer that is a securities transaction covered under §546(e). The provision explicitly equates the transfer that the trustee may otherwise avoid with the transfer that, under the safe harbor, the trustee may not avoid. In other words, to qualify for protection under the securities safe harbor, §546(e) provides that the otherwise avoidable transfer itself be a transfer that meets the safe-harbor criteria.

Thus, the statutory language and the context in which it is used all point to the transfer that the trustee seeks to avoid as the relevant transfer for consideration of the §546(e) safe-harbor criteria.

B

The statutory structure also reinforces our reading of §546(e). *See Hall v. United States* (2012) (looking to statutory structure in interpreting the Bankruptcy Code). As the Seventh Circuit aptly put it, the Code "creates both a system for avoiding transfers and a safe harbor from avoidance—logically these are two sides of the same coin." *See also Fidelity Financial Services, Inc. v. Fink* (1998) ("Section 546 of the Code puts certain limits on the avoidance powers set forth elsewhere"). Given that structure, it is only logical to view the pertinent transfer under §546(e) as the same transfer that the trustee seeks to avoid pursuant to one of its avoiding powers.

As noted in Part I–A, supra, the substantive avoidance provisions in Chapter 5 of the Code set out in detail the criteria that must be met for a transfer to fall within the ambit of the avoiding powers. These provisions, as Merit admits, "focus mostly on the characteristics of the transfer that may be avoided." Brief for Petitioner 28. The trustee, charged with exercising those avoiding powers, must establish to the satisfaction of a court that the transfer it seeks to set aside meets the characteristics set out under the substantive avoidance provisions. Thus, the trustee is not free to define the transfer that it seeks to avoid in any way it chooses. Instead, that transfer is necessarily defined by the carefully set out criteria in the Code. As FTI itself recognizes, its power as trustee to define the transfer is not absolute because "the transfer identified must satisfy the terms of the avoidance provision the trustee invokes." Brief for Respondent 23.

Accordingly, after a trustee files an avoidance action identifying the transfer it seeks to set aside, a defendant in that action is free to argue that the trustee failed to properly identify an avoidable transfer under the Code, including any available arguments concerning the role of component parts of the transfer. If a trustee properly identifies an avoidable transfer, however, the court has no reason to examine the relevance of component parts when considering a limit to the avoiding power, where that limit is defined by reference to an otherwise avoidable transfer, as is the case with §546(e), see Part II–A, supra.

In the instant case, FTI identified the purchase of Bedford Downs' stock by Valley View from Merit as the transfer that it sought to avoid. Merit does not contend that FTI improperly identified the Valley View–to–Merit transfer as the transfer to be avoided, focusing instead on whether FTI can "ignore" the component parts at the safe-harbor inquiry. Absent that argument, however, the Credit Suisse and Citizens Bank component parts are simply irrelevant to the analysis under §546(e). The focus must remain on the transfer the trustee sought to avoid.

III

A

The primary argument Merit advances that is moored in the statutory text concerns the 2006 addition of the parenthetical "(or for the benefit of)" to §546(e). Merit contends that in adding the phrase "or for the benefit of" to the requirement that a transfer be "made by or to" a protected entity, Congress meant to abrogate the 1998 decision of the Court of Appeals for the Eleventh Circuit in In re Munford, Inc., 98 F.3d 604, 610 (1996) (per curiam), which held that the §546(e) safe harbor was inapplicable to transfers in which a financial institution acted only as an intermediary. Congress abrogated Munford, Merit reasons, by use of the disjunctive "or," so that even if a beneficial interest, i.e., a transfer "for the benefit of" a financial institution or other covered entity, is sufficient to trigger safe harbor protection, it is not necessary for the financial institution to have a beneficial interest in the transfer for the safe harbor to apply. Merit thus argues that a transaction "by or to" a financial institution such as Credit Suisse or Citizens Bank would meet the requirements of §546(e), even if the financial institution is acting as an intermediary without a beneficial interest in the transfer.

Merit points to nothing in the text or legislative history that corroborates the proposition that Congress sought to overrule Munford in its 2006 amendment. There is a simpler explanation for Congress' addition of this language that is rooted in the text of the statute as a whole and consistent with the interpretation of §546(e) the Court adopts. A number of the substantive avoidance provisions include that language, thus giving a trustee the power to avoid a transfer that was made to "or for the benefit of" certain actors. See §547(b)(1) (avoiding power with respect to preferential transfers "to or for the benefit of a creditor"); §548(a)(1) (avoiding power with respect to certain fraudulent transfers "including any transfer to or for the benefit of an insider ..."). By adding the same language to the §546(e) safe harbor, Congress ensured that the scope of the safe harbor matched the scope of the avoiding powers. For example, a trustee seeking to avoid a preferential transfer under §547 that was made "for the benefit of a creditor," where that creditor is a covered entity under §546(e), cannot now escape application of the §546(e) safe harbor just because the transfer was not "made by or to" that entity.

Nothing in the amendment therefore changed the focus of the §546(e) safe-harbor inquiry on the transfer that is otherwise avoidable under the substantive avoiding powers. If anything, by tracking language already included in the substantive avoidance provisions, the amendment reinforces the connection between the inquiry under §546(e) and the otherwise avoidable transfer that the trustee seeks to set aside.

Merit next attempts to bolster its reading of the safe harbor by reference to the inclusion of securities clearing agencies as covered entities under §546(e). Because a securities clearing agency is defined as, inter alia, an intermediary in payments or deliveries made in connection with securities transactions, see 15 U.S.C. §78c(23)(A) and 11 U.S.C. §101(48) (defining "securities clearing agency" by reference to the Securities Exchange Act of 1934), Merit argues that the §546(e) safe harbor must be read to protect intermediaries without reference to any beneficial interest in the transfer. The contrary interpretation, Merit contends, "would run afoul of the canon disfavoring an interpretation of a statute that renders a provision ineffectual or superfluous." Brief for Petitioner 25.

Putting aside the question whether a securities clearing agency always acts as an intermediary without a beneficial interest in a challenged transfer—a question that the District Court in Seligson found presented triable issues of fact in that case—the reading of the statute the Court adopts here does not yield any superfluity. Reading §546(e) to provide that the relevant transfer for purposes of the safe harbor is the transfer that the trustee seeks to avoid under a substantive avoiding power, the question then becomes whether that transfer was "made by or to (or for the benefit of)" a covered entity, including a securities clearing agency. If the transfer that the trustee seeks to avoid was made "by" or "to" a securities clearing agency (as it was in Seligson), then §546(e) will bar avoidance, and it will do so without regard to whether the entity acted only as an intermediary. The safe harbor will, in addition, bar avoidance if the transfer was made "for the benefit of" that securities clearing agency, even if it was not made "by" or "to" that entity. This reading gives full effect to the text of §546(e).

B

In a final attempt to support its proposed interpretation of §546(e), Merit turns to what it perceives was Congress' purpose in enacting the safe harbor. Specifically, Merit contends that the broad language of §546(e) shows that Congress took a "comprehensive approach to securities and commodities transactions" that "was prophylactic, not surgical," and meant to "advanc[e] the interests of parties in the finality of transactions." Brief for Petitioner 41–43. Given that purported broad purpose, it would be incongruous, according to Merit, to read the safe harbor such that its application "would depend on the identity of the investor and the manner in which it held its investment" rather than "the nature of the transaction generally." Id., at 33. Moreover, Merit posits that Congress' concern was plainly broader than the risk that is posed by the imposition of avoidance liability on a securities industry entity because Congress provided a safe harbor not only for transactions "to" those entities (thus protecting the entities from direct financial liability), but also "by" these entities to non-covered entities. See Reply Brief 10–14. And, according to Merit, "[t]here is no reason to believe that Congress was troubled by the possibility that transfers by an industry hub could be unwound but yet was unconcerned about trustees' pursuit of transfers made through industry hubs." Id., at 12–13 (emphasis in original).

Even if this were the type of case in which the Court would consider statutory purpose, here Merit fails to support its purposivist arguments. In fact, its perceived purpose is actually contradicted by the plain language of the safe harbor. Because, of course, here we do have a good reason to believe that Congress was concerned about transfers "by an industry hub" specifically: The safe harbor saves from avoidance certain securities transactions "made by or to (or for the benefit of)" covered entities. See §546(e). Transfers "through" a covered entity, conversely, appear nowhere in the statute. And although Merit complains that, absent its reading of the safe harbor, protection will turn "on the identity of the investor and the manner in which it held its investment," that is nothing more than an attack on the text of the statute, which protects only certain transactions "made by or to (or for the benefit of)" certain covered entities.

For these reasons, we need not deviate from the plain meaning of the language used in §546(e).

IV

For the reasons stated, we conclude that the relevant transfer for purposes of the §546(e) safe harbor is the same transfer that the trustee seeks to avoid pursuant to its substantive avoiding powers. Applying that understanding of the safe-harbor provision to this case yields a straightforward result. FTI, the trustee, sought to avoid the $16.5 million Valley View–to–Merit transfer. FTI did not seek to avoid the component transactions by which that overarching transfer was executed. As such, when determining whether the §546(e) safe harbor saves the transfer from avoidance liability, i.e., whether it was "made by or to (or for the benefit of) a ... financial institution," the Court must look to the overarching transfer from Valley View to Merit to evaluate whether it meets the safe-harbor criteria. Because the parties do not contend that either Valley View or Merit is a "financial institution" or other covered entity, the transfer falls outside of the §546(e) safe harbor. The judgment of the Seventh Circuit is therefore affirmed, and the case is remanded for further proceedings consistent with this opinion.

It is so ordered.

NOTES

1. *Merit Management* appears to interpret §546(e) as a personal defense held by certain transferees (financial institutions and financial participants) rather than a generally applicable defense to certain otherwise avoidable transfers. Why privilege large financial institutions to retain fraudulent transfers and preferences that others similarly situated must disgorge even in the absence of a systemic effect on securities markets generally? How does *Merit Management* interact with the general understanding (and apparent plain language) of §550 authorizing recovery of transfers not only from the beneficiary of a transfer but from an initial transferee of that transfer? *Compare Levit v. Ingersoll Rand Fin. Corp. (In re Deprizio)* 874 F.2d 1186 (7th Cir. 1989), discussed at TENTH EDITION, pp. 313-314.

2. Consider the strategy adopted by unsecured creditors in *In re Tribune Company Fraudulent Conveyance Litigation,* 818 F.3d 98 (2d Cir. 2016), as a workaround to a broad interpretation of §546(e). In that case, the plan provided that upon confirmation, the state law fraudulent transfer rights ordinarily exercised by the bankruptcy trustee revested in the creditors who held those rights prebankruptcy. Those creditors, in turn, assigned the rights so revested to a trust that would pursue the actions under state law for the benefit of all former unsecured creditors. The trust argued that §546(e) would not apply to its fraudulent transfer claims because no analogue to §546(e) applied under applicable state law and the bankruptcy trustee or other bankruptcy estate representative who would be subject to the §546(e) defense would not be the plaintiff in this litigation. Judge Winter for the Second Circuit found that this scheme to avoid the safe harbor defense was preempted by §546(e), writing:

> "In the context of the Code, however, any such process is a glaring anomaly. Section 548(a)(1)(A) vests trustees with a federal claim to avoid the very transfers attacked by appellants' state law claims—but only on an intentional fraud theory. There is little apparent reason to limit trustees et al. to intentional fraud claims while not extinguishing constructive fraud claims but rather leaving them to be brought later by individual creditors. In particular, enforcement of the intentional fraud claim is undermined if creditors can later bring state law, constructive fraudulent conveyance claims involving the same transfers. Any trustee would have grave difficulty negotiating more than a nominal settlement in the federal action if it cannot preclude state claims attacking the same transfers but not requiring a showing of actual fraudulent intent. ...

> Staying ordinary state law, constructive fraudulent conveyance claims by individual creditors while the trustee deliberates is a rational method of avoiding piecemeal litigation and ensuring an equitable distribution of assets among creditors. ... However, the scheme described by appellants

does not resemble this method either in simplicity or in the equitable treatment of creditors.

To rationalize these anomalies, appellants speculate as to—more accurately, imagine—a deliberate balancing of interests by Congress. They argue that Congress wanted to balance the need for certainty and finality in securities markets, recognized in Section 546(e), against the need to maximize creditors' recoveries, recognized in various other provisions. Congress did so, they argue, by limiting only the avoidance powers of trustees et al., not those of individual creditors (save for the stay), in Section 546(e) because actions by trustees et al. are a greater threat to securities markets than are actions by individual creditors. Resp. & Reply Br. of Pls.–Appellants–Cross–Appellees 71. That greater threat results from the fact that a trustee's power of avoidance is funded by the debtor's estate, see 11 U.S.C. §§327, 330, supported by national long-arm jurisdiction, *see* Fed. R. Bankr.P. 7004(d), (f), and can be used to avoid the entirety of a transfer, *Tronox Inc. v. Anadarko Petroleum Corp. (In re Tronox Inc.)*, 464 B.R. 606, 615–17 (Bankr.S.D.N.Y.2012) (citing *Moore v. Bay*, 284 U.S. 4, 52 S.Ct. 3, 76 L.Ed. 133 (1931)). Creditors, in turn, have no such funding, are limited by state jurisdictional rules, and can sue only for their individual losses. ...

However, the balance described above is an ex post explanation of a legal scheme that appellants must first construct, and then justify as rational, because it is essential to their claims. Although they argue that the scheme was deliberately constructed by Congress, that argument lacks any support whatsoever in the legislative deliberations that led to Section 546(e)'s enactment. ...

The broad language used in Section 546(e) protects transactions rather than firms, reflecting a purpose of enhancing the efficiency of securities markets in order to reduce the cost of capital to the American economy. *See* Bankruptcy of Commodity and Securities Brokers: Hearings Before the Subcomm. on Monopolies and Commercial Law of the Comm. on the Judiciary, 47th Cong. 239 (1981) (statement of Bevis Longstreth, Commissioner, SEC) (explaining that, with 546(e), the Bankruptcy Code's "preference, fraudulent transfer and stay provisions can be interpreted to apply in harmful and costly ways to customary methods of operation essential to the securities industry"). As noted, central to a highly efficient securities market are methods of trading securities through intermediaries. Section 546(e)'s protection of the transactions consummated through these intermediaries was not intended as protection of politically favored special interests. Rather, it was sought by the SEC—and corresponding provisions by the CFTC, see Bankruptcy Act Revision: Hearings on H.R. 31 and H.R. 32 Before the Subcomm. on Civil & Constitutional Rights of the H. Comm. on the Judiciary, 94th Cong., Supp.App. Pt. 4, 2406 (1976)—in order to protect investors from the disruptive effect of after-the-fact unwinding of securities transactions.

A lack of protection against the unwinding of securities transactions would create substantial deterrents, limited only by the copious imaginations of able lawyers, to investing in the securities market. The effect of appellants' legal theory would be akin to the effect of eliminating the limited liability of investors for the debts of a corporation: a reduction of capital available to American securities markets.

In re Tribune Company Fraudulent Conveyance Litigation, 818 F.3d 98, 115-123 (2d Cir. 2016).

3. Does Judge Winter's preemption analysis survive *Merit Management*? The broad interpretation of §546(e) adopted by Judge Winter seems to have been rejected in *Merit Management*. Nevertheless, the targets of at least some of the avoidance actions in *Tribune* may well qualify as "financial institutions," §101(22A), or "financial participants," §101(22A), and therefore be entitled to assert the safe harbor even after *Merit Management*. Assume that the *Tribune* transfers to financial institutions are not avoidable under §546(e) even after *Merit Management*. Is Judge Winter still correct that the §546(e) defense applies to actions pursued by a trust asserting state law causes of action revested in creditors pursuant to the terms of a confirmed Chapter 11 plan?

4. In the most recent round of *Tribune* litigation, a district court judge in the Southern District of New York held that Tribune *itself* was a "financial institution" for the purposes of §546(e). In re Tribune Company Fraudulent Conveyance Litigation, 2019 WL 1771786 (S.D.N.Y. April 23, 2019). Although the definition of "financial participant" could not include Tribune, since it refers to an entity that enters into an agreement with the debtor and thus excludes the debtor, the definition of "financial institution" includes a "customer" of a "bank" or "trust company." Because Tribune engaged CTC to act as depository for the transactions in question, and was therefore a "customer" of CTC, a bank and a trust company, Tribune qualified as a financial institution under §546(e). Having concluded that the transactions in question were protected by §546(e), Judge Denise Cote refused to permit the Litigation Trustee for the Tribune Litigation Trust to amend his complaint to add federal constructive fraud allegations. She brushed aside the Trustee's invocation of *Merit Management*, pointing out that the Supreme Court explicitly declined to interpret the definition of "financial institution," since the parties in *Merit Management* did not argue that it applied to the debtor or the ultimate recipients of the transfers. *Merit Management*, 138 S.Ct. at 890 n.2. If this new *Tribune* ruling is any indication, *Merit Management* has not ended the ongoing controversies over the precise scope of §546(e).

5.   CORPORATE DISTRIBUTIONS AS FRAUDULENT TRANSFERS

6.   REASONABLY EQUIVALENT VALUE IN CORPORATE TRANSACTIONS

7.   LEVERAGED BUYOUTS

   a.   Insolvency

   b.   The Innocent Shareholder Defense

    c.   Special Defenses for Counterparties to Swaps, Derivatives, Repurchase Agreements and Other Financial Contracts

> Insert at the end of Textual Note at p. 373:

The leading case on the scope of the §546(e) safe harbor is now *Merit Management Group LP v. FTI Consulting, Inc*, 138 S.Ct. 883 (2018), reprinted in this 2019 SUPPLEMENT at p. 40.

D. THE STRONG-ARM CLAUSE

Readers may be interested in a recent strong-arm power decision by the First Circuit, *In re* Financial Oversight and Management Board for Puerto Rico, 914 F.3d 694 (1st Cir. 2019), cert. pending sub nom. Financial Oversight and Management Board for Puerto Rico v. Andalusian Global Designated Activity Co., Sup. Ct. No. 18-1389 (filed Apr. 30, 2019). We do not offer further comment because one of the Casebook authors is a member of the Financial Oversight and Management Board for Puerto Rico, one of the parties in the case.

CHAPTER 8

EQUITABLE SUBORDINATION AND SUBSTANTIVE CONSOLIDATION

A. EQUITABLE SUBORDINATION

1. CLAIMS OF INSIDERS

    a.   Inequitable Conduct

    b.   Undercapitalization

    c.   Recharacterization

> Insert at end of textual note on p. 394

In recent years, a circuit split has developed over the question whether to apply federal or state law to recharacterization, with five circuits applying federal law and two applying state law. The Supreme Court was poised to resolve the split, having granted *certiorari* to review *PEM Entities LLC v. Levin,* No. 15-1669 (4th Cir., *unpub. per curium*, Aug. 12, 2016) (following *Dornier*) but the Court subsequently dismissed the writ as improvidently granted. 138 S.Ct. 41 (2017).

2. CLAIMS OF NONINSIDERS

B. SUBSTANTIVE CONSOLIDATION

CHAPTER 9

THE CONSUMER DEBTOR IN CHAPTERS 7 AND 13

A. INTRODUCTION TO CONSUMER BANKRUPTCY

1. BACKGROUND

> Insert at p. 424 at the end of the first full paragraph:

Since BAPCPA, many commentators have suggested a need to review the landscape in consumer bankruptcy cases. To that end, in 2016, the American Bankruptcy Institute appointed a Commission on Consumer Bankruptcy to study 48 different aspects of consumer bankruptcy. The ABI Commission issued its Final Report in April 2019, making numerous recommendations to both Congress and the courts on key issues in consumer bankruptcy, including student loan debt, remedies for discharge violations, and the means test and eligibility for Chapter 7 and Chapter 13 bankruptcy. *See* www.consumer commission.abi.org.

2. PRIVATE SECTOR DEBT RELIEF

3. BANKRUPTCY RELIEF

B. THE CONSUMER DEBTOR IN CHAPTER 7 BEFORE BAPCPA

C. BAPCPA

1. INTRODUCTION

2. THE MEANS TEST

3. DEBTOR'S DUTIES

4.   DUTIES OF DEBTOR'S ATTORNEY AND U.S. TRUSTEE

     a.   Attorneys

     b.   Debt Relief Agencies

     c.   Advertising

     d.   U.S. Trustee

> Insert at p. 456 at the end of carryover paragraph:

For an analysis of decisions made by the U.S. Trustee under §704(b)(2), *see* Laura B. Bartell, *Section 704(b)(2)—The Back Door into Chapter 7 for the Above-Median Debtor*, 92 AM. BANKR. L.J. 489, 492 (2018) (concluding that "the United States trustees are utilizing their discretion under §704(b)(2) to provide access to Chapter 7 to those debtors whose financial circumstances differ from those reflected in the mathematical computations used to determine the presumption of abuse ….").

     e.   Audits

5.   MANDATORY CREDIT COUNSELING

D.   CHAPTER 13 AS AN ALTERNATIVE FOR THE CONSUMER DEBTOR

1.   AN OVERVIEW OF CHAPTER 13

2.   ELIGIBILITY FOR CHAPTER 13

3.   REPEATED DISCHARGES AND FILINGS

> Insert at p. 464 after *Curry* citation:

See also In re Smith, 910 F.3d 576, 591 (1st Cir. 2018) ("Based on the provision's text, the statutory context, and Congress's intent in enacting BAPCPA, we hold that §362(c)(3)(A) terminates the entire automatic stay—as to actions against the debtor, the debtor's property, and property of the bankruptcy estate—after thirty days for second-time filers.").

4.   COMMENCING A CHAPTER 13 CASE

5.   PROPERTY OF THE ESTATE

a.   Role of Property of the Estate

> Insert at p. 467 at the end of Section D.5.a.:

One issue frequently faced by a Chapter 13 debtor is whether a lender who repossessed, but did not sell, the debtor's vehicle prepetition must automatically turn over the vehicle upon the Chapter 13 filing under §542 of the Bankruptcy Code or whether the lender may maintain possession and the "status quo" without violating the automatic stay of §362 of the Bankruptcy Code. *See* discussion *supra* SUPPLEMENT Chapter 2, Section A.2.b., pp. 3, Note 3.

b.   Conversion to Chapter 7

> Insert at p. 468 at the end of the carryover paragraph:

The United States Supreme Court addressed this issue and gave effect to the language of §348(f) in *Harris v. Viegelahn*, 135 S. Ct. 1829, 1837 (2015) (undistributed funds constituting debtor's wages and held by Chapter 13 trustee at the time of conversion must be returned to the debtor and cannot be distributed to creditors in the bankruptcy case). *See also, e.g., Dep't of Soc. Servs., Div. of Child Support Enf't v. Webb*, 908 F.3d 941, 946 (4th Cir. 2018) (addressing similar issue in the context of dismissal and explaining that "[s]ection 1326(a)(2) plainly states that when the bankruptcy court does not confirm a plan, the Chapter 13 trustee 'shall return' post-petition payments to the debtor.").

6.   THE PLAN

E.   DISCHARGE

1.   COMPLETE PAYMENT DISCHARGE

> Insert at p. 489 at the end of the carryover paragraph:

Moreover, a debtor's election to pay a mortgage outside of the plan may preclude the discharge of that debt if the debtor defaults on the mortgage payments. *See In re Mildred*, 909 F.3d 1306 (11th Cir. 2018) (mortgage debt paid outside plan was not "provided for" under plan and not subject to discharge under §1328(a)). For a discussion of payments outside of the Chapter 13 plan, *see* TENTH EDITION Section D.6.e.

2.   HARDSHIP DISCHARGE

F. REAFFIRMATION OF DISCHARGED DEBTS

G. SECURED CLAIMS IN PERSONAL PROPERTY

H. SECURED CLAIMS IN DEBTOR'S RESIDENCE

1. MODIFICATION OF HOME MORTGAGES

> Insert at p. 514 at the end of Problem:

See also In re Lister, 593 B.R. 587, 594 (Bankr. S.D. Ohio 2018) (examining different approaches to analyzing mixed-use property in the context of §1322 and adopting "the view that the anti-modification provision applies if the security interest in the real property includes the debtor's principal residence").

2. MODIFICATION OF WHOLLY UNSECURED HOME LOANS

3. THE HOME LOAN CRISIS

4. CURE OF DEFAULTS

5. THREE-TO-FIVE YEAR LIMITATION

CHAPTER 10

OPERATING THE DEBTOR & PROPOSING A PLAN

A. INTRODUCTION

B. MANAGEMENT AND CONTROL

C. OPERATING THE BUSINESS FROM PETITION TO CONFIRMATION

1. INTRODUCTION

2. USE OF DEPOSIT ACCOUNTS AND OTHER CASH COLLATERAL

3. OBTAINING CREDIT

a. Critical Vendors

> Add new Note 5 to Notes at pp. 547-48 following *Matter of Kmart Corporation*:

5. The Supreme Court, in the following passage from *Czyzewski v. Jevic Holding Corp.*, 137 S.Ct. 973 (2017), distinguished the unlawful structured dismissal before it from "interim" critical vendor orders and appears to have approved in *dicta* such orders notwithstanding deviations from strict compliance with bankruptcy priorities when the order serves other important bankruptcy related purposes:

> "Courts, for example, have approved "first-day" wage orders that allow payment of employees' prepetition wages, "critical vendor" orders that allow payment of essential suppliers' prepetition invoices, and "roll-ups" that allow lenders who continue financing the debtor to be paid first on their prepetition claims. See *Cybergenics*; D. Baird, *Elements of Bankruptcy* 232–234 (6th ed. 2014); Roe, 99 Va. L. Rev., at 1250–1264. In doing so, these courts have usually found that the distributions at issue would "enable a successful reorganization and make even the disfavored creditors better off." *In re Kmart Corp.* (7th Cir. 2004) (discussing the justifications for critical-vendor orders); see also *Toibb v. Radloff* (US 1991) (recognizing "permitting business debtors to reorganize and restructure their debts in order to revive the debtors' businesses" and "maximizing the value of the bankruptcy estate" as purposes of the Code). By way

of contrast, in a structured dismissal like the one ordered below, the priority-violating distribution is attached to a final disposition; it does not preserve the debtor as a going concern; it does not make the disfavored creditors better off; it does not promote the possibility of a confirmable plan; it does not help to restore the *status quo ante*; and it does not protect reliance interests. In short, we cannot find in the violation of ordinary priority rules that occurred here any significant offsetting bankruptcy-related justification."
137 S. Ct. at 985-86.

Although *Jevic* seems to suggest that priority violation in the context of critical vendor orders may be permissible, at least if even disfavored creditors benefit, strict compliance with that standard may constitute a significant tightening of critical vendor practices. For example, in *In re Pioneer Health Services, Inc.*, 570 B.R. 228 (Bankr. S.D. Miss. 2017), the court refused, post-*Jevic*, to authorize critical vendor payments to three independent-contractor doctors at a hospital on the ground that the doctors could be held to have violated the automatic stay if they withheld their post-petition services.

   b.   Rights of Administrative Claimants

   c.   Rights of Prepetition Creditors

   d.   Cross-Collateralization

> Add new Note 3 to Notes at pp. 564-65 following *Matter of Saybrook Mfg. Co.*:

3. The Supreme Court, in the following passage from *Czyzewski v. Jevic Holding Corp.*, 137 S.Ct. 973 (2017), distinguished the unlawful structured dismissal before it from "interim" financing orders and appears to have implicitly approved "roll-ups" in such orders that authorize deviations from strict compliance with bankruptcy priorities when the order serves other important bankruptcy related purposes:

"Courts, for example, have approved "first-day" wage orders that allow payment of employees' prepetition wages, "critical vendor" orders that allow payment of essential suppliers' prepetition invoices, and "roll-ups" that allow lenders who continue financing the debtor to be paid first on their prepetition claims. See *Cybergenics*; D. Baird, Elements of Bankruptcy 232–234 (6th ed. 2014); Roe, 99 Va. L. Rev., at 1250–1264. In doing so, these courts have usually found that the distributions at issue would "enable a successful reorganization and make even the disfavored creditors better off." *In re Kmart Corp.* (7th Cir. 2004) (discussing the justifications for critical-vendor orders); *see also Toibb v. Radloff* (1991) (recognizing "permitting business debtors to reorganize and restructure their debts in order to revive the debtors' businesses" and "maximizing the value of the bankruptcy estate" as purposes of the Code). By way of contrast, in a structured dismissal like the one ordered below, the priority-violating distribution is attached to a final disposition; it does not preserve the debtor as a going concern; it does not make the disfavored creditors better off; it does not promote the possibility of a confirmable plan; it does

not help to restore the status quo ante; and it does not protect reliance interests. In short, we cannot find in the violation of ordinary priority rules that occurred here any significant offsetting bankruptcy-related justification."
137 S. Ct. at 985-86.

D. PROPOSING THE PLAN

1. INTRODUCTION

2. EXCLUSIVITY

3. ACCEPTANCE OF THE PLAN

> Add new Note 7 at p. 586 following *In re Figter, Ltd*:

7. *Figter* and *DBSD* deal with the issue of the good faith of the voting creditor. But the plan proponent that solicits the votes also has an obligation to "propose [the plan] in good faith and not by means forbidden by law." §1129(a)(3). In Garvin v. Cook Inves. NW, SPNWY, LLC, 2019 U.S. App. LEXIS 13235 (9th Cir. May 2, 2019), the U.S. Trustee objected to confirmation of an otherwise confirmable consensual Chapter 11 plan because the debtor as plan proponent did not comply with §1129(a)(3). The Debtor owned commercial real estate in the State of Washington and had leased one of its properties to a company that sold marijuana. Although the State of Washington had legalized the sale of marijuana, it remains a serious federal felony, albeit one that the Department of Justice has chosen as a matter of prosecutorial discretion not to enforce. The U.S. Trustee appealed arguing that a plan predicated on carrying on a business that was illegal under federal law did not satisfy §1129(a)(3). The Ninth Circuit rejected this argument adopting a narrow interpretation of the good faith requirement:

> Whether the Amended Plan was confirmable depends on whether §1129(a)(3) forbids confirmation of a plan that is proposed in an unlawful manner as opposed to a plan with substantive provisions that depend on illegality, an issue of first impression in the Ninth Circuit...[W]e conclude that §1129(a)(3) directs courts to look only to the proposal of a plan, not the terms of the plan...[C]onfirmation of a plan does not insulate debtors from prosecution for criminal activity, even if that activity is part of the plan itself. There is thus no need to "convert the bankruptcy judge into an ombudsman without portfolio, gratuitously seeking out possible 'il-

legalities' in every plan," a result that would be "inimical to the basic function of bankruptcy judges in bankruptcy proceedings." Because the Amended Plan was lawfully proposed, the Bankruptcy Court correctly concluded that it met the requirements of 11 U.S.C. §1129(a).

Garvin v. Cook Inves. NW, SPNWY, LLC, 2019 U.S. App. LEXIS at 13235 (9th Cir. May 2, 2019) (citations omitted).

4.   IMPAIRMENT OF CLAIMS OR INTERESTS

> Note pp. 586-88:

Note in connection with the carryover paragraph in the Textual Note that the Ninth Circuit has now found that its prior *Entz-White* decision is no longer tenable in light of the subsequent amendment to §1123(d), and, accordingly, reinstatement under §1124 now requires payment of contractual default interest to the extent enforceable under otherwise applicable nonbankruptcy law. *In re New Investments, Inc.*, 840 F.3d 1137 (9th Cir. 2016).

> Append to Note on Impairment of Claims or Interests on p. 588:

In re Ultra Petroleum Corporation

United States Court of Appeals, Fifth Circuit, 2019.
913 F.3d 533.

■ OLDHAM, Circuit Judge:

These bankruptcy proceedings arise from exceedingly anomalous facts. The debtors entered bankruptcy insolvent and now are solvent. That alone makes them rare. But second, the debtors accomplished their unlikely feat by virtue of a lottery-like rise in commodity prices. The combination of these anomalies makes these debtors as rare as the proverbial rich man who manages to enter the Kingdom of Heaven.

The key legal question before us is whether the rich man's creditors are "impaired" by a plan that paid them everything allowed by the Bankruptcy Code. The bankruptcy court said yes. In that court's view, a plan impairs a creditor if it refuses to pay an amount the Bankruptcy Code independently disallows. In reaching that conclusion, the bankruptcy court split from the only court of appeals to address the question, every reported bankruptcy court decision on the question, and the leading treatise discussing the question. We reverse and follow the monolithic mountain of authority holding the Code—not the reorganization plan—defines and limits the claim in these circumstances.

Because the bankruptcy court saw things differently, it ordered the debtors to pay certain creditors a contractual Make-Whole Amount and postpetition interest at a contractual default rate. We vacate and remand those determinations for reconsideration.

I.

Ultra Petroleum Corporation ("Petroleum") is an oil and gas exploration and production company. To be more precise, it's a holding company. Petroleum's subsidiaries—UP Energy Corporation ("Energy") and Ultra Resources, Inc. ("Resources")—do the exploring and producing. Resources took on debt to finance its operations. Between 2008 and 2010, Resources issued unsecured notes worth $1.46 billion to various noteholders. And in 2011, it borrowed another $999 million under a Revolving Credit Facility. Petroleum and Energy guaranteed both debt obligations.

In 2014, crude oil cost well over $100 per barrel. But then Petroleum's fate took a sharp turn for the worse. Only a year and a half later, a barrel cost less than $30. The world was flooded with oil; Petroleum and its subsidiaries were flooded with debt. On April 29, 2016, the companies voluntarily petitioned for reorganization under Chapter 11. No one argues the companies filed those petitions in bad faith.

During bankruptcy proceedings, however, oil prices rose. Crude oil approached $80 per barrel, and the Petroleum companies became solvent again. So, the debtors proposed a rare creature in bankruptcy—a reorganization plan that (they said) would compensate the creditors in full. As to creditors with claims under the Note Agreement and Revolving Credit Facility (together, the "Class 4 Creditors"), the debtors would pay three sums: the outstanding principal on those obligations, pre-petition interest at a rate of 0.1%, and post-petition interest at the federal judgment rate. Accordingly, the debtors elected to treat the Class 4 Creditors as "unimpaired." Therefore, they could not object to the plan. §1126(f).

The Class 4 Creditors objected just the same. They insisted their claims were impaired because the plan did not require the debtors to pay a contractual Make-Whole Amount and additional post-petition interest at contractual default rates.

Under the Note Agreement, prepayment of the notes triggers the Make-Whole Amount. That amount is designed "to provide compensation for the deprivation of" a noteholder's "right to maintain its investment in the Notes free from repayment." A formula defines the Make-Whole Amount as the amount by which "the Discounted Value of the Remaining Scheduled Payments with respect to the Called Principal" exceeds the notes' "Called Principal." Remaining scheduled payments include "all payments of [the] Called Principal and interest … that would be due" after prepayment (if the notes had never been prepaid). And the discounted value of those payments is keyed to a "Reinvestment Yield" of 0.5% over the total anticipated return on comparable U.S. Treasury obligations.

Under the Note Agreement, petitioning for bankruptcy automatically renders the outstanding principal, any accrued interest, and the Make-Whole Amount "immediately due and payable." Failure to pay immediately triggers interest at a default rate of either 2% above the normal rate set for the note at issue or 2% above J.P. Morgan's publicly announced prime rate, whichever is greater.

The Revolving Credit Facility does not contain a make-whole provision. But it does contain a similar acceleration clause that made the outstanding principal and any accrued interest "automatically … due and payable" as soon as Resources petitioned for bankruptcy. And it likewise provides for interest at a contractual default rate—2% above "the rate otherwise applicable to [the] Loan"—if Resources delayed paying the accelerated amount.

Under these two agreements, the creditors argued the debtors owed them an additional $387 million—$201 million as the Make-Whole Amount and $186 million in post-petition interest. Both sides chose to kick the can down the road. Rather than force resolution of the impairment issue at the plan-confirmation stage, the parties stipulated the bankruptcy court could resolve the dispute by deeming the creditors unimpaired and confirming the proposed plan. Meanwhile, the debtors would set aside $400 million to compensate the Class 4 Creditors if necessary "to render [the creditors] Unimpaired." The bankruptcy court agreed and confirmed the plan.

After confirmation, the parties (and the bankruptcy court) turned back to the question of impairment. The debtors acknowledged the plan did not pay the Make-Whole Amount or provide post-petition interest at the contractual default rates. But they insisted the Class 4 Creditors were not "impaired" because federal (and state) law barred them from recovering the Make-Whole Amount and entitled them to receive post-petition interest only at the federal judgment rate.

The Bankruptcy Code provides that a class of claims is not impaired if "the [reorganization] plan ... leaves unaltered the legal, equitable, and contractual rights to which such claim ... entitles the holder." §1124(1). Elsewhere the Code states that a court should disallow a claim "to the extent that [it seeks] unmatured interest." §502(b)(2). The debtors argued the Make-Whole Amount qualified as unmatured interest. But even if it didn't, they said, it was an unenforceable liquidated damages provision under New York law. In either case, something other than the reorganization plan itself—the Bankruptcy Code or New York contract law—prevented the Class 4 Creditors from recovering the disputed amounts.

    ...

The bankruptcy court rejected the premise that it must bake in the Code's provisions before asking whether a claim is impaired. Instead it concluded unimpairment "requires that [creditors] receive all that they are entitled to under state law." In other words, if a plan does not provide the creditor with all it would receive under state law, the creditor is impaired even if the Code disallows something state law would otherwise provide outside of bankruptcy. So, the bankruptcy court asked only whether New York law permits the Class 4 Creditors to recover the Make-Whole Amount (concluding it does), and whether the Code limits the contractual post-petition interest rates (concluding it does not). It never decided whether the Code disallows the Make-Whole Amount as "unmatured interest" under §502(b)(2) or what §726(a)(5)'s "legal rate" of interest means. It ordered the debtors to pay the Make-Whole Amount and post-petition interest at the contractual rates to make the Class 4 Creditors truly unimpaired.

    ...

II.

We consider first whether a creditor is "impaired" by a reorganization plan simply because it incorporates the Code's disallowance provisions. We think not.

A.

Chapter 11 lays out a framework for proposing and confirming a reorganization plan. Confirmation of the plan "discharges the debtor from any debt that arose before the date of such confirmation." §1141(d)(1). Because discharge affects a creditor's rights, the Code generally requires a debtor to vie for the creditor's vote first. §1129(a)(8). And when it does, the creditor may vote to accept or reject the plan. §1126(a). But the creditor's right to vote disappears when the plan doesn't actually affect his rights. If the creditor is "not impaired under [the] plan," he is "conclusively presumed to have accepted" it. §1126(f). The question, then, is whether the Class 4 Creditors were "impaired" by the plan.

Let's start with the statutory text. Section 1124(1) says "a class of claims or interests" is not impaired if "the plan ... leaves unaltered the [claimant's] legal, equitable, and contractual rights." The Class 4 Creditors spill ample ink arguing their rights have been altered. But that's both undisputed and insufficient. The plain text of §1124(1) requires that "the plan" do the altering. We therefore hold a creditor is impaired under §1124(1) only if "the plan" itself alters a claimant's "legal, equitable, [or] contractual rights."

The only court of appeals to address the question took the same approach. In *In re PPI Enterprises*, a landlord (creditor) argued the reorganization plan of his former tenant (debtor) impaired his claim because it did not pay him the full $4.7 million of rent he was owed over the life of the lease. The Third Circuit disagreed. Because the Bankruptcy Code caps lease-termination damages under §502(b)(6), the plan merely reflected the Code's disallowance. At the end of the day, "a creditor's claim outside of bankruptcy is not the relevant barometer for impairment; we must examine whether the plan itself is a source of limitation on a creditor's legal, equitable, or contractual rights." Ibid. It simply did not matter the landlord "might have received considerably more if he had recovered on his leasehold claims before [the debtor] filed for bankruptcy." Id. at 205. The debtor's plan gave the landlord everything the law entitled him to once bankruptcy began, so he was unimpaired.

Decisions from bankruptcy courts across the country all run in the same direction. [Citations omitted.] All agree that "[i]mpairment results from what the plan does, not what the [bankruptcy] statute does." *Solar King*.

The creditors cannot point to a single decision that suggests otherwise. That's presumably why COLLIER'S treatise states the point in unequivocal terms: "Alteration of Rights by the Code Is Not Impairment under Section 1124(1)." "We are always chary to create a circuit split." *United States v. Graves* (5th Cir. 2018). That's especially true "in the context of bankruptcy, where uniformity is sufficiently important that our Constitution authorizes Congress to establish 'uniform laws on the subject of bankruptcies throughout the United States.' " *In re Marciano*, (9th Cir. 2013) (Ikuta, J., dissenting). We refuse to create one today.

B.

The Class 4 Creditors' counterarguments do not move the needle. First, they focus on §1124(1)'s use of the word "claim." They note the Code elsewhere speaks of "allowed claims." See, e.g., §§506(a)(1), 506(a)(2), 510(c)(1), 1126(c). Then they suggest the absence of "allowed" in §1124(1) means "claim" there refers to the claim before the Code's disallowance provisions come in and trim its edges.

But the broader statutory context cuts the other way. Section 1124 is not just (or even primarily) about the allowance of claims. It is about rights—the "legal, equitable, and contractual rights to which [the] claim ... entitles the holder." §1124(1). That means we judge impairment after considering everything that defines the scope of the right or entitlement—such as a contract's language or state law. See In re Energy Future Holdings Corp. (Bankr. D. Del. 2015); §502(b)(1). Even the bankruptcy court recognized this to some extent because it asked whether New York law permitted the Noteholders to recover the Make-Whole Amount. "The Bankruptcy Code itself is a statute which, like other statutes, helps to define the legal rights of persons." *Solar King.*

Finding no help in §1124(1)'s statutory text, the Class 4 Creditors turn to the legislative history of a different provision. In 1994, Congress repealed §1124(3), which provided that a creditor's claim was not impaired if the plan paid "the *allowed amount* of such claim." §1124(3) (1988) (emphasis added). This proves, they say, that disallowance should now play no role in the impairment analysis.

Even for those who think legislative history can be relevant to statutory interpretation, this particular history is not. It does not say that every disallowance causes impairment. Rather, Congress repealed §1124(3) in response to a specific bankruptcy court decision. In re New Valley Corp. (Bankr. D.N.J. 1994). That decision held unsecured creditors who received their allowed claims from a solvent debtor, but who did not receive post-petition interest, were unimpaired. In debating the proposed repeal of §1124(3), the House Judiciary Committee singled out *New Valley* by name as the justification for the repeal. See H.R. Rep. No. 103-835 (1994) (citing *New Valley* and explaining the intent to repeal §1124(3) "to preclude th[e] unfair result" of "den[ying] the right to receive post petition interest"). It is noteworthy the committee report does not cite other bankruptcy cases—such as *Solar King*—that addressed Code impairment under §1124(1). That is why the Third Circuit rejected appellees' legislative-history argument in *PPI* and held the repeal of §1124(3) "does not reflect a sweeping intent by Congress to give impaired status to creditors more freely outside the postpetition interest context." 324 F.3d at 207 (noting the committee report cited *New Valley* but not *Solar King*).

Next, the Class 4 Creditors attempt to distinguish *PPI*. True, that case involved disallowance under §502(b)(6), not §502(b)(2). But that's a distinction without a difference. *See In re W.R. Grace & Co.* (Bankr. D. Del. 2012); *Energy Future*. Section 502 states that "the court ... shall allow [a] claim in [the requested] amount, except to the extent that" any one of nine conditions apply. If any of the enumerated conditions applies, the court shall not allow the relevant portion of the claim. *PPI* reasoned that where one of those conditions applies, the Code—not the plan—impairs the creditors' claims. That reasoning applies with equal force to §502(b)(2).

The Class 4 Creditors (like the bankruptcy court) also point to the mechanics of Chapter 11 discharge to suggest the plan itself, not the Code, is doing the impairing. They note the Code's disallowance provisions are carried into effect only if the plan is confirmed, and "confirmation of the plan ... discharges the debtor from any debt that arose before" confirmation. §1141(d). In one sense, plan confirmation limits creditors' claims for money by discharging underlying debts. But in another sense, the Code limits the creditors' claims for money and imposes substantive and procedural requirements for plan confirmation. The Class 4 Creditors' argument thus begs the critical question: What is doing the work here? We agree with *PPI*, every reported decision identified by either party, and COLLIER'S treatise. Where a plan refuses to pay funds disallowed by the Code, the Code—not the plan—is doing the impairing.

III.

That leaves the question whether the Code disallows the creditors' claims for the Make-Whole Amount and post-petition interest at the contractual default rates specified in the Note Agreement and the Revolving Credit Facility. The bankruptcy court never reached either question. The parties nevertheless urge us to reach them now. The creditors say their contracts entitle them to both amounts, and that their contracts should be honored under bankruptcy law's longstanding "solvent-debtor" exception. The debtors argue no such exception exists in modern bankruptcy law. And the debtors further argue both claims are governed by the Bankruptcy Code, not the pre-Code law or the parties' contracts.

[The court's discussion of the historical pre-Code understanding of the solvent-debtor exception is omitted.]

C.

...

1.

We start with whether the Make-Whole Amount is disallowed by §502(b)(2). That Code provision requires a bankruptcy court to disallow a claim "to the extent that [it seeks] unmatured interest." §502(b)(2). Our precedent in turn defines §502(b)(2)'s "unmatured interest" by looking to economic realities, not trivial formalities. *In re Pengo Indus., Inc.*, (5th Cir. 1992) ("economic reality," "economic fact," "economic equivalent"). Section 502(b)(2) thus disallows any claim that is the economic equivalent of unmatured interest.

The debtors make a compelling argument the Make-Whole Amount is one such disallowed claim. We are persuaded by three aspects of the debtors' argument.

First, the Make-Whole Amount is the economic equivalent of "interest." The purpose of a make-whole provision "is to compensate the lender for lost interest." 4 COLLIER, supra, ¶ 502.03[a]; *see In re MPM Silicones, L.L.C.* (2d Cir. 2017) (The "make-whole premium was intended to ensure that [noteholders] received additional compensation to make up for the interest they would not receive if the Notes were redeemed prior to their maturity date."); *In re Energy Future Holdings Corp.* (3d Cir. 2016) (similar). So too here. The Make-Whole Amount is calculated by subtracting the accelerated principal from the discounted value of the future principal and interest payments. That captures the value of the interest the Noteholders would have eventually received if the Notes had not been prepaid. *See In re Doctors Hosp. of Hyde Park* (Bankr. N.D. Ill. 2014).

Second, the interest for which the Make-Whole Amount compensates was "unmatured" when the debtors filed their Chapter 11 petitions. Section 502(b)'s disallowance provisions apply "as of the date of the filing of the petition." On that day, the debtors did not owe the Make-Whole Amount or the underlying interest. The Note Agreement's acceleration clause doesn't change things because it operates as an *ipso facto* clause by keying acceleration to, among other things, the debtor's decision to file a bankruptcy petition. *See In re Lehman Bros. Holdings* (Bankr. S.D.N.Y. 2010); Ipso Facto Clause, BLACK'S LAW DICTIONARY 957 (Del. 10th ed. 2014). And the parties agree that an ipso facto clause is unenforceable. "[W]hether interest is considered to be matured or un-matured for the purpose of [§502(b)(2)] is to be determined without reference to any ipso facto bankruptcy clause in the agreement creating the claim." 4 COLLIER, supra, ¶ 502.03[b]; see H.R. Rep. No. 95-595 (1977). The Class 4 Creditors' only response is the acceleration clause is not an ipso facto clause because it could also be triggered by something other than a bankruptcy peti-tion. They cite nothing for that proposition.

Third, those decisions taking a different view are unpersuasive. Some courts have concluded §502(b)(2) does not cover make-whole provisions on the assumption "they fully mature pursuant to the provisions of the contract." *In re Outdoor Sports Headquarters* (Bankr. S.D. Ohio 1993); *see In re Skyler Ridge* (Bankr. C.D. Cal. 1987). But *ipso facto* clauses count for nothing when deciding maturity under §502(b)(2). Others have concluded make-whole pro-visions are better viewed as liquidated damages, rather than unmatured interest. But those categories are not mutually exclusive.

The Class 4 Creditors' most persuasive response is that none of these ar-guments applies to a solvent debtor. First, they try the "absolute priority rule," insisting it bars a solvent debtor from paying stockholders any surplus before fully compensating its creditors. That is only half right. For starters, the abso-lute priority rule applies when asking whether a plan is "fair and equitable" in a cram-down scenario. §1129(b)(1). It is not a freewheeling exception requir-ing a debtor to pay amounts the Code otherwise prohibits. But more im-portantly, the rule itself builds in the Code's disallowance provisions. It stands for the proposition that a plan "may not allocate any property whatsoever to any junior class … unless all senior classes consent, or unless such senior clas-ses receive property equal in value to the full amount of their *allowed claims*." 7 COLLIER, supra, ¶ 1129.03[a][i] (emphasis added). Thus, the Class 4 Credi-tors simply beg the question whether §502(b)(2) disallows the Make-Whole Amount; if it does, the absolute priority rule takes that into account.

Their second argument fares better: If the pre-Code solvent-debtor excep-tion survives in the background of the Code, then the Class 4 Creditors have a point. English bankruptcy law gave the creditors of a solvent debtor the "right to interest wherever there is a contract for it." 1 COOKE, THE BANKRUPT LAWS (6th ed. 1812); *accord Bromley*, 26 Eng. Rep. at 50–52. And it appears undis-puted the Class 4 Creditors would have a contractual right outside of bank-ruptcy to the interest specified in the Make-Whole Amount. Therefore, the pre-Code solvent-debtor exception would operate as a carve-out from §502(b)(2)'s general bar on unmatured interest—in much the same way the exception oper-ated as a carve-out from the pre-Code rule barring contract interest after the commission date.

The only question then is whether the pre-Code solvent-debtor exception survives the enactment of §502(b)(2). Congress carefully incorporated some pre-Code principles but not others. And those principles it did incorporate, Congress sometimes modified. It might be true Congress chose not to codify the solvent-debtor rule as an absolute exception to §502(b)(2). *See, e.g., Ron Pair Enters*; *Timbers of Inwood* On the other hand, we sometimes presume congressional silence leaves undisturbed certain long-established bankruptcy principles. *See, e.g., Midlantic Nat'l Bank v. N.J. Dep't of Envtl. Prot.* (1986); *Kelly v. Robinson* (1986). The bankruptcy court's resolution of the Code-im-pairment question prevented it from considering these arguments. "[M]indful that we are a court of review, not of first view," we will not make the choice ourselves. *Cutter v. Wilkinson* (2005).

One last note on our remand of the Make-Whole Amount. Much of the pre-Code law regarding solvent debtors—including our 1911 decision in *Johnson*—appears motivated by concerns over bad-faith filings. That is, courts worried that without the solvent-debtor exception, solvent debtors would seek bankruptcy protection in bad faith simply to avoid paying their debts. And many of the creditors' arguments before our Court have the same flavor. But Chapter 11 addresses this problem by creating a motion-to-dismiss procedure for bad-faith filings. See §1112(b). And as far as the record reveals, the Class 4 Creditors never availed themselves of that procedure or complained it was insufficient. That is presumably because the debtors are both solvent and good-faith filers. We trust the bankruptcy court on remand also will consider what effect (if any) §1112(b) has on the solvent-debtor exception (if any exists).

* * *

As we have explained, Code impairment is not the same thing as plan impairment. Because the bankruptcy court found otherwise, it did not address whether the Code disallows the Make-Whole Amount or post-petition interest, and if not, how much the debtors must pay the Class 4 Creditors. To secure plan confirmation, the parties stipulated the debtors would do whatever is necessary to make the creditors unimpaired. The bankruptcy court, therefore, must make that stipulation a reality. For that reason and others explained above, we REVERSE in part, VACATE in part, and REMAND for further proceedings consistent with this opinion.

5. CLASSIFICATION OF CLAIMS

> Insert as new Note 7 on p. 605:

7. Note that in connection with the discussion of §1129(a)(10) (requiring at least one consenting impaired class) in Note 5 following *Matter of Greystone III Joint Venture* that the Ninth Circuit has now weighed in on whether the one-consenting class requirement is applied on a per-plan or per-debtor basis in considering joint reorganization plans involving affiliated entities. In *JPMCC 2007-C1 Grasslawn Lodging, LLC v. Transwest Resort Props. (Matter of Transwest Resort Props.)*, 881 F.3d 724 (9th Cir. 2018), the court determined that the per-plan approach was the correct approach. Judge Friedland concurring in *Transwest* noted that the per-plan approach in the context of the case amounted to a de facto substantive consolidation but considered any objection based on the propriety of that consolidation waived.

CHAPTER 11

CONFIRMING A CHAPTER 11 PLAN

A. FEASIBILITY

B. TREATMENT OF PRIORITY CLAIMS

C. TREATMENT OF SECURED CLAIMS

1. §1129(b)(2)(A) STANDARDS FOR CRAMDOWN

    a. Deferred Cash Payments

    > After Notes following *Till v. SCS Credit Corp.* at p. 632 add the following:

Matter of MPM Silicones, LLC

United States Court of Appeals, Second Circuit, 2017.
874 F.3d 787 (as amended), *cert. denied*, 138 S.Ct. 2653.

■ PARKER, Circuit Judge:

Three groups of creditors separately appeal a judgment of the United States District Court of the Southern District of New York (Briccetti, J.) affirming the confirmation of Debtors' Chapter 11 reorganization plan by the U.S. Bankruptcy Court (Drain, J.). The creditors argue that the plan improperly eliminated or reduced the value of notes they held. Debtors argue that the plan was properly confirmed and that these appeals should be dismissed as equitably moot. With one exception, we conclude that the plan confirmed by the bankruptcy court and affirmed by the district court comports with the provisions of Chapter 11. We remand so that the bankruptcy court can address the single deficiency we identify with the proceedings below which is the process for determining the proper interest rate under the cramdown provision of Chapter 11. We decline to dismiss these appeals as equitably moot.

I

MPM, a leading producer of silicone, faced serious financial problems after it took on significant new debt obligations beginning in the mid-2000s. Following these debt issuances, MPM was substantially overleveraged, and ultimately filed a petition under Chapter 11. The four relevant classes of notes issued by MPM are as follows:

Subordinated Notes. In 2006, MPM issued $500 million in subordinated unsecured notes (the "Subordinated Notes") pursuant to an indenture (the "2006 Indenture"). Appellant U.S. Bank is the indenture trustee for the Subordinated Notes. In 2009 MPM issued secured second-lien notes and offered the

Subordinated Notes holders the option of exchanging their notes for the newly-issued second-lien notes. The second-lien notes were offered at a 60% discount but were secured. Holders of $118 million of the Subordinated Notes accepted the offer, leaving $382 million in unsecured Subordinated Notes outstanding.

Second-Lien Notes. In 2010, MPM issued approximately $1 billion in "springing" second-lien notes (the "Second-Lien Notes"). The Second-Lien Notes were to be unsecured until the $118 million of previously exchanged Subordinated Notes were redeemed, at which point the "spring" in the lien would be triggered. Once triggered, the Second-Lien Notes would then (but only then) obtain a security interest in the Debtor's collateral. The exchanged Subordinated Notes were redeemed in November 2012, at which point the trigger occurred and the Second-Lien Notes became secured with second-priority liens junior to other pre-existing liens on the Debtors' collateral. A primary issue on this appeal is whether the Second-Lien Notes have priority over the Subordinated Notes.

Senior-Lien Notes. In 2012, MPM again issued more debt, this time in the form of two classes of senior secured notes. Specifically, MPM issued $1.1 billion in first-lien secured notes (the "First-Lien Notes"), and $250 million in 1.5-lien secured notes (the "1.5-Lien Notes," and, with the First-Lien Notes, the "Senior-Lien Notes"). Appellants BOKF and Wilmington Trust are the indenture trustees for the First-Lien Notes and 1.5-Lien Notes, respectively. Pursuant to the governing indentures (the "2012 Indentures"), the Senior-Lien Notes were to be repaid in full by their maturity date of October 15, 2020. They carried fixed interest rates of 8.875% and 10%, respectively. The 2012 Indentures also called for the recovery of a "make-whole" premium if MPM opted to redeem the notes prior to maturity. Because the Second-Lien Notes and the Senior-Lien Notes are secured by the same collateral, the holders of those notes executed an intercreditor agreement (the "Intercreditor Agreement"), which provided that the Senior-Lien Notes stood in priority to the Second-Lien Notes as to their respective liens, but that each was junior to pre-existing liens on MPM's collateral. Other primary issues on this appeal are whether the Senior-Lien Note holders are entitled to the make-whole adjustment and the cramdown interest rate they are entitled to if their Notes are replaced under the Plan.

II

After these notes were issued, MPM experienced significant financial problems. In April 2014, MPM filed a petition under Chapter 11 and ultimately submitted a reorganization plan to the bankruptcy court. Several elements of that Plan are at issue on these appeals. The Plan provided for (i) a 100% cash recovery of the principal balance and accrued interest on the Senior-Lien Notes; (ii) an estimated 12.8%-28.1% recovery on the Second-Lien Notes in the form of equity in the reorganized Debtors; but (iii) no recovery on the Subordinated Notes.

The Plan also gave the Senior-Lien Notes holders the option of (i) accepting the Plan and immediately receiving a cash payment of the outstanding principal and interest due on their Notes (without a make-whole premium), or (ii) rejecting the Plan, receiving replacement notes "with a present value equal to the Allowed amount of such holder's [claim]," and then litigating in the bankruptcy court issues including whether they were entitled to the make-whole premium and the interest rate on the replacement notes. The Senior-Lien Notes holders rejected the Plan, and, thus, elected the latter option.

The appellants here—the Subordinated Notes holders and the Senior-Lien Notes holders—opposed the Plan. (The Second-Lien Notes holders unanimously accepted it.) The Subordinated Notes holders, who were to receive nothing, contended that, under relevant indenture provisions, their Notes were not subordinate to the Second-Lien Notes holders and, consequently, they were entitled to some recovery. The Senior-Lien Notes holders opposed the Plan on the ground that the replacement notes they received did not provide for the make-whole premium, and carried a largely risk-free interest rate that failed to comply with the Code because it was well below ascertainable market rates for similar debt obligations and thus was not fair and equitable because it failed to give them the present value of their claim.

Despite these objections, the bankruptcy court confirmed the Plan following a four-day hearing. Confirmation was facilitated by Chapter 11's "cramdown" provision, which allows a bankruptcy court to confirm a reorganization plan notwithstanding non-accepting classes if the plan "does not discriminate unfairly, and is fair and equitable, with respect to each class of claims or interests that is impaired under, and has not accepted, the plan." 11 U.S.C. §1129(b)(1).

The bankruptcy court concluded that the Plan was fair to the Subordinated Notes holders, despite no recovery, because the 2006 Indenture called for their subordination to the Second-Lien Notes. It held the plan was fair to the Senior-Lien Notes holders because the 2012 Indentures did not require payment of the make-whole premium in the bankruptcy context and because the interest rate on the proposed replacement notes, even though well below a "market" rate, was determined by a formula that complied with the Code's cramdown provision.

The bankruptcy court's confirmation order triggered an automatic 14-day stay during which Debtors could not consummate the Plan. See Fed. R. Bankr. p. 3020(e). Appellants aggressively took advantage of this period and attempted to block the implementation of the Plan. Specifically, prior to the expiration of the automatic stay, appellants moved in the bankruptcy court to extend the stay pending their appeal of the confirmation order, which the court denied. They then promptly moved the district court for a stay, which was also denied. Appellants then appealed the denial of the stay to this Court, and we dismissed the appeal for lack of jurisdiction. Despite these efforts, the Debtors contend this appeal is equitably moot, a contention with which we do not agree.

The appellants appealed the confirmation order to the district court which affirmed the bankruptcy court's confirmation order. The district court essentially agreed with the bankruptcy court, concluding that: (i) the relevant indentures unambiguously prioritize the Second-Lien Notes over the Subordinated Notes; (ii) the below market interest rate selected by the bankruptcy court complied with the Code; and (iii) under their indentures, the Senior-Lien Notes holders are not entitled to the make-whole premium in the context of a bankruptcy. The Subordinated Notes holders, the First-Lien Notes holders, and the 1.5-Lien Notes holders separately appealed.

...

IV

...

B

As a consequence of rejecting the Plan, the Senior-Lien Notes holders received replacement notes which pay out their claim over time. The Code permits debtors to make such "deferred cash payments" to secured creditors (i.e., to "cramdown"). 11 U.S.C. §1129(b)(2)(A)(i)(II). However, those payments must ultimately amount to the full value of the secured creditors' claims. Id. To ensure the creditor receives the full present value of its secured claim, the deferred payments must carry an appropriate rate of interest. See *Rake v. Wade* (U.S.1993).

The rate selected by the lower courts for the Senior-Lien Note holders' replacement notes was based on the "formula" rate. The bankruptcy court selected interest rates of 4.1% and 4.85%, respectively, which were largely risk-free rates slightly adjusted for appropriate risk factors. It is not disputed that this rate is below market in comparison with rates associated with comparable debt obligations. The Debtors defend the application of the "formula" method on the ground that it is required by the plurality opinion in the Chapter 13 case of *Till v. SCS Credit Corp.* (U.S. 2004).

The Senior-Lien Notes holders contend that because this rate is too low, the Plan is not "fair and equitable" as required by §1129(b). They argue that the lower courts should have applied a market rate of interest which is the rate MPM would pay to a contemporaneous sophisticated arms-length lender in the open market. The Senior-Lien Notes holders argued in the bankruptcy court that such a market exists and would generate interest in the 5-6+% range.[7]

The bankruptcy court rejected this approach, and concluded that a cramdown interest rate should "not take market factors into account." Viewing itself as "largely governed by the principles enunciated by the plurality opinion in [*Till*]," it concluded that the proper rate was what the plurality in Till referred to as the "formula" or "prime-plus" rate (discussed more fully below). The district court agreed. The Senior-Lien Notes holders argue on appeal that the lower courts erred in concluding that the Till plurality opinion is wholly applicable to this Chapter 11 proceeding. In substantial part, we agree.

At issue in *Till* was a Chapter 13 debtor's sub-prime auto loan, carrying an interest rate of 21% and providing the creditor with a $4,000 secured claim. As with Chapter 11, Chapter 13 allows debtors to provide secured creditors with future property distributions (such as deferred cash payments) whose total "value, as of the effective date of the plan, ... is not less than the allowed amount of such claim." 11 U.S.C. §1325(a)(5)(B)(ii). The question became, as here, how to calculate the interest on the deferred payments such that the creditor would receive the full value of its claim. No single interest-calculation

---

[7] Debtors' reorganization plan proposed interest rates of 3.6% and 4.09%. However, the bankruptcy court concluded that those rates should be increased by 0.5% and 0.75%, respectively, in light of the fact that the base interest rate was pegged to the Treasury rate, rather than the prime rate (which reflects additional risk). On appeal to the district court, the Senior-Lien Notes holders argued the bankruptcy court erred in not requiring the prime rate, an argument the district court rejected. The Senior-Lien Notes holders do not press this argument here.

method secured a majority vote on the Court, resulting in a plurality opinion endorsing the "formula" method.

The "formula" approach endorsed by the *Till* plurality instructs the bankruptcy court to begin with a largely risk-free interest rate, specifically, the "national prime rate ... which reflects the financial market's estimate of the amount a commercial bank should charge a creditworthy commercial borrower to compensate for the opportunity costs of the loan, the risk of inflation, and the relatively slight risk of default." The bankruptcy court should then hold a hearing to determine a proper plan-specific risk adjustment to that prime rate "at which the debtor and any creditors may present evidence." Id. Using this approach, "courts have generally approved adjustments [above the prime rate] of 1% to 3%." Id.[8]

The *Till* plurality arrived at the "formula" rate after rejecting a number of alternative methods relied on by the lower courts. Significantly, it rejected methods relying on purported "market" rates of interest because those rates "must be high enough to cover factors, like lenders' transactions costs and overall profits, that are no longer relevant in the context of court-administered and court-supervised cramdown loans." The plurality then identified the only factors it viewed as relevant in properly ensuring that the sum of deferred payments equals present value: (i) the time-value of money; (ii) inflation; and (iii) the risk of non-payment. The plurality concluded that the "formula" or "prime-plus" method best reflects those considerations.

Although *Till* involved a Chapter 13 petition, the plurality intimated that the "formula" method might be applicable to rate calculations made pursuant to other similarly worded Code provisions. In fact, it cited the Chapter 11 cramdown provision, 11 U.S.C. §1129(b)(2)(A)(i)(II), among many other provisions, when it noted that "[w]e think it likely that Congress intended bankruptcy judges and trustees to follow essentially the same approach when choosing an appropriate interest rate under any of these [Code] provisions."

Despite that language, however, the plurality made no conclusive statement as to whether the "formula" rate was generally required in Chapter 11 cases. And, notably, the plurality went on to state, in the opinion's much-discussed footnote 14, that the approach it felt best applied in the Chapter 13 context may not be suited to Chapter 11. Specifically, in that footnote, the Court stated that in Chapter 13 cramdowns "there is no free market of willing cramdown lenders." It continued: "[i]nterestingly, the same is not true in the Chapter 11 context, as numerous lenders advertise financing for Chapter 11 debtors in possession. Thus, when picking a cramdown rate in a Chapter 11 case, it might make sense to ask what rate an efficient market would produce." Id.[9]

Many courts have relied on footnote 14 to conclude that efficient market rates for cramdown loans cannot be ignored in Chapter 11 cases. Most notably,

---

[8] Here, the bankruptcy court applied risk adjustments of 2.0% and 2.75%, which it added to the Treasury rate of 2.1% to arrive at interest rates of 4.1% and 4.85%, respectively. Debtors assert in their briefing that the Treasury rate dropped by approximately 0.2% between the confirmation date and the plan's effective date, which thereby further lowered their notes' interest rate. 15-1682 Br. of Appellee at 11 n.3.

[9] The Supreme Court has not subsequently spoken about the interest-calculation method to be applied in a Chapter 11 case. Nor have we.

the Sixth Circuit, "tak[ing] [its] cue from Footnote 14" of the *Till* plurality, adopted a two-part process for selecting an interest rate in Chapter 11 cramdowns:

> [T]he market rate should be applied in Chapter 11 cases where there exists an efficient market. But where no efficient market exists for a Chapter 11 debtor, then the bankruptcy court should employ the formula approach endorsed by the *Till* plurality.

In re American HomePatient, Inc. (6th Cir. 2005). In applying this rule, courts have held that markets for financing are 'efficient' where, for example, "they offer a loan with a term, size, and collateral comparable to the forced loan contemplated under the cramdown plan." *In re Texas Grand Prairie Hotel Realty, L.L.C.* (5th Cir. 2013).[10]

We adopt the Sixth Circuit's two-step approach, which, in our view, best aligns with the Code and relevant precedent. We do not read the Till plurality as stating that efficient market rates are irrelevant in determining value in the Chapter 11 cramdown context. And, disregarding available efficient market rates would be a major departure from long-standing precedent dictating that "the best way to determine value is exposure to a market." *Bank of Am. Nat'l Trust and Sav. Ass'n v. 203 N. LaSalle St. P'ship,* (U.S. 1999) (assessing a Chapter 11 cramdown); see also *United States v. 50 Acres of Land* (U.S.1984) ("fair market value" is "what a willing buyer would pay in cash to a willing seller"). In *Bank of America*, the Court noted that "one of the Code's innovations [was] to narrow the occasions for courts to make valuation judgments," and expressed a "disfavor for decisions untested by competitive choice ... when some form of market valuation may be available."

The Senior-Lien Notes holders presented expert testimony in the bankruptcy court that, if credited, would have established a market rate. This evidence showed that if the Senior-Lien Noteholders were to have approved the Plan and accepted a cash-out payment for their notes, MPM would have had to secure exit financing to cover the lump-sum payment. In preparation for that possible eventuality (which did not come to pass in light of the Senior-Lien Notes holders' rejection of the Plan), MPM went out into the market seeking lenders to provide that financing. Those lenders quoted MPM rates of interest ranging between 5 and 6+%.

At these rates, the First-Lien Note holders contend that they would have received around $150 million more than the Plan offered, Br. of First-Lien Appellant 25, 33. The 1.5-Lien Note holders claim that the interest rate chosen by the lower courts led them to receive notes "valued by the market at less than 93 cents on the value of the secured claims," Br. of 1.5-Lien Appellant 20.[11] The Plan was objectionable to the Senior-Lien Notes holders because, in essence, it required them to lend Debtors a significant sum of money and receive a much lower rate of interest than any other lender would have received for offering the same loan to MPM on the open market.

---

[10] Numerous courts, included in this Circuit, have followed the *American HomePatient* approach. *See, e.g.*, *In re 20 Bayard Views, LLC* (E.D.N.Y. 2011) (collecting cases and deciding to "follow the majority approach" first outlined in *American HomePatient*).

[11] The Senior-Lien Notes holders offered evidence that the market price for their notes dropped, respectively, from 101.375% and 104.000% six days prior to the bankruptcy court's oral decision, to 94.375% and 92.563% nine days after that decision.

When dealing with a sub-prime loan in the Chapter 13 context, "value" can be elusive because the market is not necessarily efficient and the borrower is typically unsophisticated. However, where, as here, an efficient market may exist that generates an interest rate that is apparently acceptable to sophisticated parties dealing at arms-length, we conclude, consistent with footnote 14, that such a rate is preferable to a formula improvised by a court. See *Bank of America*; see also *In re Valenti* (2d Cir. 1997) (the goal of the cramdown rate "is to put the creditor in the same economic position that it would have been in had it received the value of its allowed claim immediately"); see also 15-1682 JA 3428 (First-Lien Notes holders' expert testifying that because the First-Lien Notes holders "are pricing it at the market ... they're being compensated for the underlying risk that they are taking," and not for any "imbedded profit").

We understand that the complexity of the task of determining an appropriate market rate will vary from case to case. In some cases the task will be straightforward, in others it will be more complex. But, at the end of the day, we have no reason to believe the task varies materially in difficulty from the myriad tasks which we regularly rely on the expertise of our bankruptcy courts to resolve.

We therefore conclude that the lower courts erred in categorically dismissing the probative value of market rates of interest. We remand so that the bankruptcy court can ascertain if an efficient market rate exists and, if so, apply that rate, instead of the formula rate.[12] We arrive at no conclusion with regard to the outcome of this inquiry.

C

[The Court's discussion of the enforceability of a pre-payment ("make-whole") provision in the senior notes is omitted].

V

[The Court's discussion of equitable mootness is omitted].

VI

To summarize, we conclude as follows:

1. The Second-Lien Notes stand in priority to the Subordinated Notes.

2. The Senior-Lien Notes holders are not entitled to the make-whole premium.

3. The lower court erred in the process it used to calculate the interest rate applicable to the replacement notes received by the Senior-Lien Notes holders. On remand, the bankruptcy court should assess whether an efficient market rate can be ascertained, and, if so, apply it to the replacement notes.

---

[12] We acknowledge that the lower courts grappled with the Senior-Lien Notes holders' evidence regarding MPM's quoted exit financing, and made express their view that the rate produced by that process may not in fact have been produced by an efficient market. Nevertheless, Judge Drain left no ambiguity that he applied the "formula" approach for Chapter 13 individual bankruptcy cases as dictated by the *Till* plurality and, in so doing, explicitly declined to consider market forces. *See id.* at ("I conclude that [the *American HomePatient*] two-step method, generally speaking, misinterprets *Till*"). Judge Briccetti agreed with this approach. As discussed, this was in error. The bankruptcy court should have the opportunity to engage the *American HomePatient* analysis in earnest.

4. We decline to dismiss any of these appeals as equitably moot.

b.   Sale of Property

c.   Indubitable Equivalence

Add new Note 4 following *Arnold & Baker Farms* at p. 650:

4. Distinguishing *Arnold & Baker Farms*, the Fourth Circuit approved a partial dirt-for-debt plan in *In re Bate Land & Timber LLC*, 877 F.3d 188 (4th Cir. 2017).

2.   §1129(b)(1) "FAIRNESS" AND NEGATIVE AMORTIZATION

3.   THE §1111(b) ELECTION

Insert after Problem, p. 659:

In re Sunnyslope Housing LP

United States Court of Appeals, Ninth Circuit, *en banc*, 2017.
859 F.3d 637 (*as amended*), *cert. denied*, 138 S. Ct. 648 (2018).

■ HURWITZ, Circuit Judge:

When a debtor, over a secured creditor's objection, seeks to retain and use the creditor's collateral in a Chapter 11 plan of reorganization through a "cram down," the Bankruptcy Code treats the creditor's claim as secured "to the extent of the value of such creditor's interest." §506(a)(1). That value is to "be determined in light of the purpose of the valuation and of the proposed disposition or use of such property."

In *Associates Commercial Corp. v. Rash*, the Supreme Court adopted a "replacement-value standard" for §506(a)(1) cram-down valuations. The Court held that replacement value, "rather than a foreclosure sale that will not take place, is the proper guide under a prescription hinged to the property's 'disposition or use.'"

In rejecting a "foreclosure-value standard," the Court also noted that foreclosure value was "typically lower" than replacement value. Today, however, we confront the atypical case. Because foreclosure would vitiate covenants requiring that the secured property—an apartment complex—be used for low-income housing, foreclosure value in this case exceeds replacement value, which is tied to the debtor's "actual use" of the property in the proposed reorganization. But we take the Supreme Court at its word and hold, as *Rash* teaches, that §506(a)(1) requires the use of replacement value rather than a hypothetical value derived from the very foreclosure that the reorganization is designed to avoid. Thus, the bankruptcy court did not err in this case in approving Sunnyslope's plan of reorganization and valuing the collateral assuming its continued use after reorganization as low-income housing.

BACKGROUND

Sunnyslope Housing Limited Partnership ("Sunnyslope") owns an apartment complex in Phoenix, Arizona. Construction funding came from three loans. Capstone Realty Advisors, LLC, provided the bulk of the funding through an $8.5 million loan with an interest rate of 5.35%, secured by a first-priority deed of trust. The Capstone loan was guaranteed by the United States Department of Housing and Urban Development ("HUD"), and funded through bonds issued by the Phoenix Industrial Development Authority. The City of Phoenix and the State of Arizona provided the balance of the funding. The City loan was secured by a second-position deed of trust, and the State loan by a third-position deed of trust.

A. The Covenants

To secure financing and tax benefits, Sunnyslope entered into five agreements:

1. To obtain the HUD guarantee, Sunnyslope signed a Regulatory Agreement requiring that the apartment complex be used for affordable housing.

2. Sunnyslope also entered into a Regulatory Agreement with the Phoenix Industrial Development Authority, requiring Sunnyslope to "preserve the tax-exempt status" of the project, and use 40% of the units for low-income housing. The agreement provided that its covenants "shall run with the land and shall bind the Owner, and its successors and assigns and all subsequent owners or operators of the Project or any interest therein." The restrictions, however, terminated on "foreclosure of the lien of the Mortgage or delivery of a deed in lieu of foreclosure."

3. The City of Phoenix required Sunnyslope to sign a Declaration of Affirmative Land Use Restrictive Covenants, mandating that 23 units be set aside for low-income families. The restriction ran with the land and bound "all future owners and operators" but, similarly, would be vitiated by foreclosure.

4. The Arizona Department of Housing required Sunnyslope to enter into a Declaration of Covenants, Conditions, and Restrictions. That 40-year agreement set aside five units for low-income residents. The agreement ran with the land and bound future owners, terminated upon foreclosure, and was expressly subordinate to the HUD Regulatory Agreement.

5. Finally, in order to receive federal tax credits, Sunnyslope agreed with the Arizona Department of Housing to use the entire complex as low-income housing. The tax credits, and restriction on use, would terminate on foreclosure.

B. The Default and its Aftermath

In 2009, Sunnyslope defaulted on the Capstone loan. As guarantor, HUD took over the loan and sold it to First Southern National Bank ("First Southern") for $5.05 million. In connection with the sale, HUD released its Regulatory Agreement. The Loan Sale Agreement confirmed, however, that the property remained subject to the other "covenants, conditions and restrictions."

First Southern began foreclosure proceedings, and an Arizona state court appointed a receiver. In December 2010, the receiver agreed to sell the complex to a third party for $7.65 million.

Before the sale could close, Sunnyslope filed a Chapter 11 petition. Over First Southern's objection, Sunnyslope sought to retain the complex in its proposed plan of reorganization, exercising the "cram-down" option in

§1129(b)(2)(A). A successful cram down allows the reorganized debtor to retain collateral over a secured creditor's objection, subject to the requirement in §506(a)(1) that the debt be treated as secured "to the extent of the value of such creditor's interest" in the collateral.

The central issue in the reorganization proceedings was the valuation of First Southern's collateral, the apartment complex. Sunnyslope asserted that the complex should be valued as low-income housing, while First Southern contended that the complex should instead be valued without regard to Sunnyslope's contractual obligations to use it as low-income housing, which would terminate upon foreclosure.

In that regard, First Southern's expert valued the complex at $7.74 million, making the "extraordinary assumption" that a foreclosure would remove any low income housing requirements. First Southern's expert also opined, however, that the value of the property was only $4,885,000 if those requirements remained in place. Sunnyslope's expert valued the property at $2.6 million with the low-income housing restrictions in place, and at $7 million without.

During its original proceeding, the bankruptcy court held that, under §506(a)(1), the value of the property was $2.6 million because Sunnyslope's plan of reorganization called for continued use of the complex as low-income housing. The court also declined to include in the valuation of the complex the tax credits available to Sunnyslope. First Southern then elected to treat its claim as fully secured under §1111(b).

The bankruptcy court subsequently confirmed the plan of reorganization, which provided for payment in full of the First Southern claim over 40 years, at an interest rate of 4.4%, with a balloon payment at the end without interest. The reorganization plan required the City and State to relinquish their liens, but provided for payment of their unsecured claims in full, albeit without interest, at the end of the 40 years.

The bankruptcy court found the plan fair and equitable under §1129(b)(1) because First Southern retained its lien, would receive an interest rate equivalent to the prevailing market rate, and could foreclose (and, therefore, obtain the property without the restrictive covenants) should Sunnyslope default. The court also found the plan feasible under §1129(a)(11), citing Sunnyslope's financial projections, and noting that "the Creditor has come in with no evidence of a lack of feasibility." The court concluded that it was more likely than not that Sunnyslope could make plan payments based on the history of comparable properties. The court also noted that, when the balloon payment came due, the property would be free of the low-income housing restrictions, making the collateral an even more valuable asset.

After confirmation, First Southern obtained a stay of the plan of reorganization from the district court pending appeal. The district court affirmed the bankruptcy court's valuation of the complex with the low-income housing restrictions in place, but held that the tax credits should also have been considered. Both parties appealed.

After First Southern unsuccessfully sought a writ from this court prohibiting the bankruptcy court from considering the district court's remand pending resolution of the appeals, the bankruptcy court valued the tax credits at $1.3 million, added that amount to its previous valuation, and reconfirmed the plan of reorganization. First Southern attempted to withdraw its §1111(b) election, but the bankruptcy court denied the request.

First Southern again appealed. The district court denied First Southern's request for a stay. Cornerstone at Camelback LLC invested $1.2 million in the complex, and the plan was funded. The district court affirmed the reorganization plan as modified. First Southern timely appealed to this court, and Sunnyslope cross-appealed.

A majority of the active judges of this court voted to grant Sunnyslope's petition for rehearing en banc.

DISCUSSION

The critical issue for decision is whether the bankruptcy court erred by valuing the apartment complex assuming its continued use after reorganization as low-income housing. In addition, First Southern contends that the plan of reorganization is neither fair and equitable nor feasible, and that the district court erred in not allowing it to withdraw its §1111(b) election.

Valuation

When a Chapter 11 debtor opts for a cram down, a creditor's claim is secured "to the extent of the value of such creditor's interest in the estate's interest in [the secured] property." §506(a)(1). The value of that claim is "determined in light of the purpose of the valuation and of the proposed disposition or use of such property." We established long ago that, "[w]hen a Chapter 11 debtor or a Chapter 13 debtor intends to retain property subject to a lien, the purpose of a valuation under section 506(a) is not to determine the amount the creditor would receive if it hypothetically had to foreclose and sell the collateral." *In re Taffi* (9th Cir. 1996) (en banc). The debtor is "in, not outside of, bankruptcy," so "[t]he foreclosure value is not relevant" because the creditor "is not foreclosing."

In *Taffi*, we noted that our decision was consistent with the approach of all but one circuit—the Fifth—which had adopted a foreclosure-value standard in *In re Rash* (5th Cir. 1996) (en banc). There, the Rashes owed $41,171 on a freight-hauler truck loan when they filed a Chapter 13 petition. They sought to retain the truck through a cram down, proposing a reorganization plan paying the creditor for the foreclosure value of the truck, which they contended was $28,500. In contrast, the creditor argued the truck should be valued at "the price the Rashes would have to pay to purchase a like vehicle," estimated at $41,000. But the Fifth Circuit disagreed and held that §506(a)(1) required the use of foreclosure value.

One year after we decided *Taffi*, the Supreme Court reversed the Fifth Circuit. The Court held, consistent with *Taffi*, that "§506(a) directs application of the replacement value standard," rather than foreclosure value. The Court stated that the value of collateral under §506(a)(1) is "the cost the debtor would incur to obtain a like asset for the same 'proposed ... use.'"

Rash stressed the instruction in §506(a)(1) to value the collateral based on its "proposed disposition or use" in the plan of reorganization. The Court emphasized that, in a reorganization involving a cram down, the debtor will continue to use the collateral, and valuation must therefore occur "in light of the proposed repayment plan reality: no foreclosure sale." The "actual use," the Court held, "is the proper guide," and replacement value is therefore "the price a willing buyer in the debtor's trade, business, or situation would pay to obtain like property from a willing seller."

Rash also teaches that the determination of replacement value by the bankruptcy court is a factual finding. We therefore review the valuation determination in this case for clear error. We find none.

The essential inquiry under *Rash* is to determine the price that a debtor in Sunnyslope's position would pay to obtain an asset like the collateral for the particular use proposed in the plan of reorganization. First Southern does not dispute that there was substantial evidence before the bankruptcy court that it would cost Sunnyslope $3.9 million to acquire a property like the apartment complex (including the tax-credits) with similar restrictive covenants requiring that it be devoted to lowincome housing.

Despite this, First Southern argues that the property should instead be valued at its "highest and best use"—housing without any low-income restrictions. But §506(a)(1) speaks expressly of the reorganization plan's "proposed disposition or use." Absent foreclosure, the very event that the Chapter 11 plan sought to avoid, Sunnyslope cannot use the property except as affordable housing, nor could anyone else. Rash expressly instructs that a §506(a)(1) valuation cannot consider what would happen after a hypothetical foreclosure—the valuation must instead reflect the property's "actual use."

First Southern attempts to distinguish *Rash* by noting that foreclosure value is greater than replacement value in this case. But *Rash* implicitly acknowledged that this outcome might occasionally be the case, and nonetheless adopted a replacement-value standard. We cannot depart from that standard without doing precisely what *Rash* instructed bankruptcy courts to avoid—assuming a foreclosure that the Chapter 11 petition prevented.

To be sure, a creditor is better off whenever the highest possible value for its collateral is chosen, and *Rash* did in fact recognize that when "a debtor keeps the property and continues to use it, the creditor obtains at once neither the property nor its value and is exposed to double risks: The debtor may again default and the property may deteriorate from extended use." But *Rash* did not adopt a rule requiring that the bankruptcy court value the collateral at the higher of its foreclosure value or replacement value. Rather, it expressly rejected the use of foreclosure value, and instead stressed the requirement in §506(a)(1) that the property be valued in light of its "proposed disposition or use." Here, the proposed disposition and use is for low-income housing; indeed, no other use is possible without foreclosure. First Southern may be exposed to an increased risk under the cram down, but that does not allow us to ignore the command of *Rash*.

First Southern also argues that the low-income housing requirements do not apply to its security because HUD released its Regulatory Agreement, and all other covenants are junior to its lien. Although the State and City liens may be subordinate to First Southern's, it is undisputed the restrictions they impose continue to run with the land absent foreclosure. Thus, they were properly considered in determining the value of the collateral.

Finally, First Southern's amici argue that valuing the collateral with the low-income restrictions in place would discourage future lending on like projects. We disagree. "[W]hile the protection of creditors' interests is an important purpose under Chapter 11, the Supreme Court has made clear that successful debtor reorganization and maximization of the value of the estate are the primary purposes." *In re Bonner Mall P'ship* (9th Cir. 1993), abrogated on other grounds by *Bullard v. Blue Hills Bank* (US 2015). Allowing the debtor to "rehabilitate the business" generally maximizes the value of the estate. And, in this case, First Southern bought the Sunnyslope loan at a substantial discount, knowing of the risk that the property would remain subject to the low-income housing requirements. Valuing First Southern's collateral with those restrictions in mind subjects the lender to no more risk than it consciously undertook.

Accordingly, we hold that the bankruptcy court did not err in valuing First Southern's collateral in the plan of reorganization assuming its continued use as affordable housing.[3]

Plan Fairness

The cram-down provision in §1129(b) requires that the reorganization plan be "fair and equitable." The secured creditor must retain its lien, §1129(b)(2)(A)(i)(I), and receive payments over time equaling the present value of the secured claim, §1129(b)(2)(A)(i)(II). Whether a plan is fair and equitable is a factual determination reviewed for clear error.

The bankruptcy court found the Sunnyslope plan fair and equitable because First Southern retained its lien and received the present value of its allowed claim over the term of the plan. There is no dispute that First Southern retained its lien, and our discussion above disposes of any contention that its secured claim was undervalued. Thus, the only remaining question is whether the bankruptcy court erred in concluding that the plan provides for payments equal to the present value of the secured claim.

The interest rate chosen must ensure that the creditor receives the present value of its secured claim through the payments contemplated by the plan of reorganization. *Till v. SCS Credit Corp.* (2004). In *Till*, a plurality endorsed the "formula approach" for calculating the appropriate interest rate, which begins with the national prime rate and adjusts up or down according to the risk of the plan's success. The creditor bears the burden of showing that the prime rate does not adequately account for the riskiness of the debtor.

First Southern argues that it is not receiving the present value of its secured claim because the interest rate adopted in the plan, 4.4%, is lower than the original rate on its loan. But we find no clear error in the bankruptcy court's determination. The bankruptcy court conducted a hearing at which it heard expert testimony, applied the *Till* test, and found that the 4.4% interest rate on the plan payments would result in First Southern's receiving the present value of its $3.9 million security over the term of the reorganization plan. The relevant national prime rate was 3.25%, and the bankruptcy court adjusted that rate upward to account for the risk of non-payment. The court also heard testimony that the market loan rate for similar properties was 4.18%. In setting the 4.4% rate, the bankruptcy court carefully explained its reasoning, noting that interest rates had decreased significantly since the Capstone loan was made. The bankruptcy

---

[3] The dissent correctly notes the statement in *Rash* that "[w]hether replacement value is the equivalent of retail value, wholesale value, or some other value will depend on the type of debtor and the nature of the property." But the very footnote in which that language appears stresses "that the replacement-value standard, not the foreclosure-value standard, governs in cram down cases." Given the Court's plain injunction that "actual use, not a foreclosure sale that will not take place, is the proper guide" to determining replacement value, a bankruptcy court surely cannot premise a §506(a) valuation on a hypothetical foreclosure. And, First Southern had no ability to sell the property free and clear of the low-income restrictions absent such a foreclosure.

court also noted that the risk to the lender had similarly decreased since then because, when the loan was made, the apartment complex had not yet been built.[4]

The bankruptcy court did not clearly err, and we affirm its determination.

Plan Feasibility

Plan confirmation also requires a finding that the debtor will not require further reorganization. §1129(a)(11). It therefore requires the debtor to demonstrate that the plan "has a reasonable probability of success." A bankruptcy court's finding of feasibility is reviewed for abuse of discretion.

The bankruptcy court did not abuse its discretion in finding the Sunnyslope plan feasible. A projection showed that Sunnyslope would be able to make plan payments, and expert testimony confirmed that the collateral would remain useful for 40 years (the term of the plan). The court also found the balloon payment feasible because it was secured by property whose value exceeded the value of the remaining First Southern claim. And the court noted that First Southern had "come in with no evidence of a lack of feasibility." It was therefore well within the bankruptcy court's discretion to find that the plan of reorganization was feasible.

The §1111(b) Election

Finally, §1111(b) of the Bankruptcy Code allows a secured creditor to elect to have its claim treated as either fully or partially secured. An election affects the treatment of the unsecured portion of the claim under the plan and the procedural protections afforded to the creditor. See, e.g., §1129(a)(7)(B). In the absence of a contrary order by the bankruptcy court, the creditor must make this election before the end of the disclosure statement hearing. Fed. R. Bankr. p. 3014.

In this case, the bankruptcy court ordered that First Southern make its §1111(b) election "calendar days after the court issues a ruling on valuation." First Southern timely did so, choosing to treat its entire claim as secured.

First Southern now argues that the bankruptcy court erred in not allowing it to make a second election after the district court remanded and required the tax credits be added to the valuation. In effect, First Southern contends that the bankruptcy court erred by not amending its scheduling order to allow the creditor a second bite at the apple. A bankruptcy court may modify a scheduling order "for cause," Fed. R. Bankr. p. 9006(b)(1), and we review its decision whether to do so for abuse of discretion. We assume without deciding that a court should modify a scheduling order to allow a creditor to change its §1111(b) election after a material alteration to the original plan. But, in this case, we agree with the district court that the only alteration in the plan—the increased valuation of the collateral—was not material to the election decision.

When First Southern made its election, the plan provided for 40 years of payments of principal and interest providing the creditor with the present value

---

[4] First Southern contends that the bankruptcy court erred by considering the chance of a second default as a credit enhancement. But if Sunnyslope defaults a second time, First Southern can foreclose and obtain a property worth more than the court's §506(a)(1) valuation. See *Till* (noting that risk can be evaluated in light of "the nature of the security").

of its $2.6 million secured claim, with a final balloon payment covering the remainder of the debt. After remand, as the district court noted, "First Southern's treatment under the plan as modified remains the same; the only difference is that its annual payments will be more and the balloon payment at the end of the 40 years will be less."

Significantly, the amended plan of reorganization did not alter the treatment of unsecured claims, which are to be paid without interest in 40 years, or immediately at five cents on the dollar. Thus, First Southern knew at the time of the initial election "the prospects of its treatment under the plan," (Fed. R. Bankr. p. 3014 advisory committee note), yet it opted to treat its entire claim as secured.

Allowing a second election would give First Southern a second chance to object to the plan, this time both as a secured and unsecured creditor and, given the potential size of the unsecured claim, the ability to prevent approval of the reorganization plan. See §1129(a)(7)(A)(ii). But this is precisely the option First Southern had at the time of its first election, when it chose to forgo having any portion of its claim treated as unsecured, instead seeking to increase the valuation of its secured claim through appeal. That gambit failed, and the bankruptcy court did not err when it rejected First Southern's attempt to turn back the clock and torpedo the plan of reorganization.

CONCLUSION

We AFFIRM the judgment of the district court.

KOZINSKI, Circuit Judge, dissenting:

Today's opinion claims to "take the Supreme Court at its word," but it fetishizes a selection of the Court's words at the expense of its logic. This cramped formalism produces a strange result: Even though the Court has told us that cramdown valuations are supposed to limit a secured creditor's risk, we've adopted a new valuation standard that turns entirely on the debtor's desires—creditors be damned. Instead of holding the valuation hostage to the debtor's "particular use," I would hold that the appropriate value is the market price of the building without restrictive covenants.[1]

The majority purports to rely on *Associates Commercial Corp. v. Rash*, but *Rash* never adopted today's strict "particular use" interpretation of replacement value. The Court was more flexible: "Whether replacement value is the equivalent of retail value, wholesale value, or some other value will depend on the type of debtor and the nature of the property." After all, the bare notion of "replacement value" isn't self-interpreting. A conservation-minded owner may prefer to see his lands stay wild. He may adopt an easement to keep them that way, and may not care that this drastically reduces the commercial value of the property. But the owner's preferences don't shape the market value of an undeveloped acre—which is what the owner who actually did buy new replacement property would have to pay.

---

[1] In this case, the price a buyer would have to pay on the market for like property may be closely approximated by "foreclosure value." That coincidence drives the majority's analysis, but it does nothing to answer the real question presented by this case: Whether the market valuation commanded by Rash turns on a debtor's idiosyncratic use of the particular property. It does not.

What interpretation of "replacement value" should we use? Unhelpfully, *Rash* offers few specifics on how the nature of the property and the debtor should affect valuation.[2] But *Rash* expressly notes that replacement value shouldn't include certain warranties and modifications that drive a wedge between private value and market value. And *Rash* was unambiguously motivated by a desire to reduce what it saw as the "double risks" that cramdowns pose for creditors: "The debtor may again default and the property may deteriorate from extended use." With these risks in mind, the *Rash* Court adopted a broad standard—the typically higher replacement value over the typically lower foreclosure value—that would give secured creditors their due protection. *See also Till v. SCS Credit Corp* (2004) (Thomas, J., concurring) (noting that creditors are "compensated in part for the risk of nonpayment through the valuation of the secured claim" because *Rash* used a "secured-creditor-friendly replacement-value standard rather than the lower foreclosure-value standard"). A moment's reflection reveals why today's holding is at odds with these motivations: The majority's valuation falls well below what the secured creditor would obtain from an immediate sale.[3]

In short, the majority has adopted a test that is not dictated by the letter of *Rash* and is contradicted by its reasoning.

---

[2] The fact that *Rash* does not adopt a strict definition of "replacement value" and offers little guidance on how to apply it has been widely appreciated by other courts and commentators. *See, e.g.,* CHARLES JORDAN TABB, LAW OF BANKRUPTCY 741 (4th ed. 2016) (describing footnote 6 of *Rash* as a "substantial opening" that has allowed a wide variety of valuation standards to flourish). I make no effort to defend *Rash*, which has been subject to abundant criticism along these lines. But I also see no reason to step beyond it, as today's majority does.

[3] In my view, much of this risk will be passed on to borrowers in the form of higher interest rates—in which case, the joke's on future Sunnyslopes. Regardless, the Supreme Court expressly held that "[a]djustments in the interest rate and secured creditor demands for more 'adequate protection' do not fully offset" the risks of cramdowns. *Rash* (quoting §361). Of course, one reason for ex-post credit risk might be *Rash* itself: It's hard for parties to bargain in the shadow of an unclear rule.

D. TREATMENT OF UNSECURED CLAIMS AND OWNERSHIP INTERESTS

1. BEST INTERESTS TEST

2. ABSOLUTE PRIORITY RULE

3. INTER-CLASS "GIVE-UPS"

> Insert after Notes following *In re DBSD North America*, p. 675:

Czyzewski v. Jevic Holding Corp.

Supreme Court of the United States, 2017.
137 S.Ct. 973.

■ Justice BREYER delivered the opinion of the Court.

Bankruptcy Code Chapter 11 allows debtors and their creditors to negotiate a plan for dividing an estate's value. But sometimes the parties cannot agree on a plan. If so, the bankruptcy court may decide to dismiss the case. §1112(b). The Code then ordinarily provides for what is, in effect, a restoration of the prepetition financial status quo. §349(b).

In the case before us, a Bankruptcy Court dismissed a Chapter 11 bankruptcy. But the court did not simply restore the prepetition status quo. Instead, the court ordered a distribution of estate assets that gave money to high-priority secured creditors and to low-priority general unsecured creditors but which skipped certain dissenting mid-priority creditors. The skipped creditors would have been entitled to payment ahead of the general unsecured creditors in a Chapter 11 *plan* (or in a Chapter 7 liquidation). The question before us is whether a bankruptcy court has the legal power to order this priority-skipping kind of distribution scheme in connection with a Chapter 11 *dismissal*.

In our view, a bankruptcy court does not have such a power. A distribution scheme ordered in connection with the dismissal of a Chapter 11 case cannot, without the consent of the affected parties, deviate from the basic priority rules that apply under the primary mechanisms the Code establishes for final distributions of estate value in business bankruptcies.

I

A

1

We begin with a few fundamentals: A business may file for bankruptcy under either Chapter 7 or Chapter 11. In Chapter 7, a trustee liquidates the debtor's assets and distributes them to creditors. In Chapter 11, debtor and creditors try to negotiate a plan that will govern the distribution of valuable assets from the debtor's estate and often keep the business operating as a going concern.

Filing for Chapter 11 bankruptcy has several relevant legal consequences. First, an estate is created comprising all property of the debtor. §541(a)(1). Second, a fiduciary is installed to manage the estate in the interest of the creditors. §§1106, 1107(a). This fiduciary, often the debtor's existing management team, acts as "debtor in possession." §§1101(1), 1104. It may operate the business, §§363(c)(1), 1108, and perform certain bankruptcy-related functions, such as seeking to recover for the estate preferential or fraudulent transfers made to other persons, §547 (transfers made before bankruptcy that unfairly preferred particular creditors); §548 (fraudulent transfers, including transfers made before bankruptcy for which the debtor did not receive fair value). Third, an "automatic stay" of all collection proceedings against the debtor takes effect. §362(a).

It is important to keep in mind that Chapter 11 foresees three possible outcomes. The first is a bankruptcy-court-confirmed plan. Such a plan may keep the business operating but, at the same time, help creditors by providing for payments, perhaps over time. See §§1123, 1129, 1141. The second possible outcome is conversion of the case to a Chapter 7 proceeding for liquidation of the business and a distribution of its remaining assets. §§1112(a), (b), 726. That conversion in effect confesses an inability to find a plan. The third possible outcome is dismissal of the Chapter 11 case. §1112(b). A dismissal typically "revests the property of the estate in the entity in which such property was vested immediately before the commencement of the case"—in other words, it aims to return to the prepetition financial status quo. §349(b)(3).

Nonetheless, recognizing that conditions may have changed in ways that make a perfect restoration of the status quo difficult or impossible, the Code permits the bankruptcy court, "for cause," to alter a Chapter 11 dismissal's ordinary restorative consequences. §349(b). A dismissal that does so (or which has other special conditions attached) is often referred to as a "structured dismissal," defined by the American Bankruptcy Institute as a

> "hybrid dismissal and confirmation order … that … typically dismisses the case while, among other things, approving certain distributions to creditors, granting certain third-party releases, enjoining certain conduct by creditors, and not necessarily vacating orders or unwinding transactions undertaken during the case."

American Bankruptcy Institute Commission To Study the Reform of Chapter 11, 2012–2014 Final Report and Recommendations 270 (2014).

Although the Code does not expressly mention structured dismissals, they "appear to be increasingly common." *Ibid.,* n. 973.

2

The Code also sets forth a basic system of priority, which ordinarily determines the order in which the bankruptcy court will distribute assets of the estate. Secured creditors are highest on the priority list, for they must receive the proceeds of the collateral that secures their debts. 11 U.S.C. §725. Special classes of creditors, such as those who hold certain claims for taxes or wages, come next in a listed order. §§507, 726(a)(1). Then come low-priority creditors, including general unsecured creditors. §726(a)(2). The Code places equity holders at the bottom of the priority list. They receive nothing until all previously listed creditors have been paid in full. §726(a)(6).

The Code makes clear that distributions of assets in a Chapter 7 liquidation must follow this prescribed order. It provides somewhat more flexibility for

distributions pursuant to Chapter 11 plans, which may impose a different ordering with the consent of the affected parties. But a bankruptcy court cannot
confirm a plan that contains priority-violating distributions over the objection
of an impaired creditor class. §§1129(a)(7), 1129(b)(2).

The question here concerns the interplay between the Code's priority rules
and a Chapter 11 dismissal. Here, the Bankruptcy Court neither liquidated the
debtor under Chapter 7 nor confirmed a Chapter 11 plan. But the court, instead
of reverting to the prebankruptcy status quo, ordered a distribution of the estate
assets to creditors by attaching conditions to the dismissal (*i.e.,* it ordered a
structured dismissal). The Code does not explicitly state what priority rules—
if any—apply to a distribution in these circumstances. May a court consequently provide for distributions that deviate from the ordinary priority rules
that would apply to a Chapter 7 liquidation or a Chapter 11 plan? Can it approve
conditions that give estate assets to members of a lower priority class while
skipping objecting members of a higher priority class?

B

In 2006, Sun Capital Partners, a private equity firm, acquired Jevic Transportation Corporation with money borrowed from CIT Group in a "leveraged
buyout." In a leveraged buyout, the buyer (B) typically borrows from a third
party (T) a large share of the funds needed to purchase a company (C). B then
pays the money to C's shareholders. Having bought the stock, B owns C. B
then pledges C's assets to T so that T will have security for its loan. Thus, if
the selling price for C is $50 million, B might use $10 million of its own money,
borrow $40 million from T, pay $50 million to C's shareholders, and then
pledge C assets worth $40 million (or more) to T as security for T's $40 million
loan. If B manages C well, it might make enough money to pay T back the $40
million and earn a handsome profit on its own $10 million investment. But, if
the deal sours and C descends into bankruptcy, beware of what might happen:
Instead of C's $40 million in assets being distributed to its existing creditors,
the money will go to T to pay back T's loan—the loan that allowed B to buy
C. (T will receive what remains of C's assets because T is now a secured creditor, putting it at the top of the priority list). Since C's shareholders receive
money while C's creditors lose their claim to C's remaining assets, unsuccess-
ful leveraged buyouts often lead to fraudulent conveyance suits alleging that
the purchaser (B) transferred the company's assets without receiving fair value
in return. See Lipson & Vandermeuse, *Stern,* Seriously: The Article I Judicial
Power, Fraudulent Transfers, and Leveraged Buyouts, 2013 Wis. L.Rev. 1161,
1220–1221.

This is precisely what happened here. Just two years after Sun's buyout,
Jevic (C in our leveraged buyout example) filed for Chapter 11 bankruptcy. At
the time of filing, it owed $53 million to senior secured creditors Sun and CIT
(B and T in our example), and over $20 million to tax and general unsecured
creditors.

The circumstances surrounding Jevic's bankruptcy led to two lawsuits.
First, petitioners, a group of former Jevic truckdrivers, filed suit in bankruptcy
court against Jevic and Sun. Petitioners pointed out that, just before entering
bankruptcy, Jevic had halted almost all its operations and had told petitioners
that they would be fired. Petitioners claimed that Jevic and Sun had thereby
violated state and federal Worker Adjustment and Retraining Notification
(WARN) Acts—laws that require a company to give workers at least 60 days'
notice before their termination. See 29 U.S.C. §2102; N.J. Stat. Ann. §34:21–

2 (West 2011). The Bankruptcy Court granted summary judgment for petition-ers against Jevic, leaving them (and *this* is the point to remember) with a judg-ment that petitioners say is worth $12.4 million. Some $8.3 million of that judgment counts as a priority wage claim under 11 U.S.C. §507(a)(4), and is therefore entitled to payment ahead of general unsecured claims against the Jevic estate.

Petitioners' WARN suit against Sun continued throughout most of the lit-igation now before us. But eventually Sun prevailed on the ground that Sun was not the workers' employer at the relevant times.

Second, the Bankruptcy Court authorized a committee representing Jevic's unsecured creditors to sue Sun and CIT. The Bankruptcy Court and the parties were aware that any proceeds from such a suit would belong not to the unsecured creditors, but to the bankruptcy estate. See §§541(a)(1), (6); *Official Comm. of Unsecured Creditors of Cybergenics Corp. v. Chinery* (3d Cir. 2003) (en banc) (holding that a creditor's committee can bring a derivative action on behalf of the estate). The committee alleged that Sun and CIT, in the course of their leveraged buyout, had "hastened Jevic's bankruptcy by saddling it with debts that it couldn't service." In 2011, the Bankruptcy Court held that the com-mittee had adequately pleaded claims of preferential transfer under §547 and of fraudulent transfer under §548.

Sun, CIT, Jevic, and the committee then tried to negotiate a settlement of this "fraudulent-conveyance" lawsuit. By that point, the depleted Jevic estate's only remaining assets were the fraudulent-conveyance claim itself and $1.7 million in cash, which was subject to a lien held by Sun.

The parties reached a settlement agreement. It provided (1) that the Bank-ruptcy Court would dismiss the fraudulent-conveyance action with prejudice; (2) that CIT would deposit $2 million into an account earmarked to pay the committee's legal fees and administrative expenses; (3) that Sun would assign its lien on Jevic's remaining $1.7 million to a trust, which would pay taxes and administrative expenses and distribute the remainder on a pro rata basis to the low-priority general unsecured creditors, *but which would not distribute any-thing to petitioners* (who, by virtue of their WARN judgment, held an $8.3 million mid-level-priority wage claim against the estate); and (4) that Jevic's Chapter 11 bankruptcy would be dismissed.

Apparently Sun insisted on a distribution that would skip petitioners be-cause petitioners' WARN suit against Sun was still pending and Sun did not want to help finance that litigation. See 787 F.3d, at 177–178, n. 4 (Sun's coun-sel acknowledging before the Bankruptcy Court that "'Sun probably does care where the money goes because you can take judicial notice that there's a pend-ing WARN action against Sun by the WARN plaintiffs. And if the money goes to the WARN plaintiffs, then you're funding someone who is suing you who otherwise doesn't have funds and is doing it on a contingent fee basis'"). The essential point is that, regardless of the reason, the proposed settlement called for a structured dismissal that provided for distributions that did not follow ordinary priority rules.

Sun, CIT, Jevic, and the committee asked the Bankruptcy Court to approve the settlement and dismiss the case. Petitioners and the U.S. Trustee objected, arguing that the settlement's distribution plan violated the Code's priority scheme because it skipped petitioners—who, by virtue of their WARN judg-ment, had mid-level priority claims against estate assets—and distributed estate money to low-priority general unsecured creditors.

The Bankruptcy Court agreed with petitioners that the settlement's distribution scheme failed to follow ordinary priority rules. But it held that this did not bar approval. That, in the Bankruptcy Court's view, was because the proposed payouts would occur pursuant to a structured dismissal of a Chapter 11 petition rather than an approval of a Chapter 11 plan. The court accordingly decided to grant the motion in light of the "dire circumstances" facing the estate and its creditors. Specifically, the court predicted that without the settlement and dismissal, there was "no realistic prospect" of a meaningful distribution for anyone other than the secured creditors. *Id.,* at 58a. A confirmable Chapter 11 plan was unattainable. And there would be no funds to operate, investigate, or litigate were the case converted to a proceeding in Chapter 7.

The District Court affirmed the Bankruptcy Court. It recognized that the settlement distribution violated ordinary priority rules. But those rules, it wrote, were "not a bar to the approval of the settlement as [the settlement] is not a reorganization plan."

The Third Circuit affirmed the District Court by a vote of 2 to 1. The majority held that structured dismissals need not always respect priority. Congress, the court explained, had only "codified the absolute priority rule ... in the specific context of plan confirmation." As a result, courts could, "in rare instances like this one, approve structured dismissals that do not strictly adhere to the Bankruptcy Code's priority scheme."

Petitioners (the workers with the WARN judgment) sought *certiorari*. We granted their petition.

II

[The Court finds that the WARN Act claimants suffered sufficient injury-in-fact and pecuniary harm to have standing to challenge the structured dismissal order].

III

We turn to the basic question presented: Can a bankruptcy court approve a structured dismissal that provides for distributions that do not follow ordinary priority rules without the affected creditors' consent? Our simple answer to this complicated question is "no."

The Code's priority system constitutes a basic underpinning of business bankruptcy law. Distributions of estate assets at the termination of a business bankruptcy normally take place through a Chapter 7 liquidation or a Chapter 11 plan, and both are governed by priority. In Chapter 7 liquidations, priority is an absolute command—lower priority creditors cannot receive anything until higher priority creditors have been paid in full. Chapter 11 plans provide somewhat more flexibility, but a priority-violating plan still cannot be confirmed over the objection of an impaired class of creditors. See §1129(b).

The priority system applicable to those distributions has long been considered fundamental to the Bankruptcy Code's operation. See H.R.Rep. No. 103–835 (1994) (explaining that the Code is "designed to enforce a distribution of the debtor's assets in an orderly manner ... in accordance with established principles rather than on the basis of the inside influence or economic leverage of a particular creditor"); Roe & Tung, *Breaking Bankruptcy Priority: How Rent-Seeking Upends The Creditors' Bargain*, 99 Va. L. Rev. 1235, 1243, 1236 (2013) (arguing that the first principle of bankruptcy is that "distribution conforms to predetermined statutory and contractual priorities," and that priority is, "quite appropriately, bankruptcy's most important and famous rule");

Markell, *Owners, Auctions, and Absolute Priority in Bankruptcy Reorganizations*, 44 Stan. L. Rev. 69, 123 (1991) (stating that a fixed priority scheme is recognized as "the cornerstone of reorganization practice and theory").

The importance of the priority system leads us to expect more than simple statutory silence if, and when, Congress were to intend a major departure. See *Whitman v. American Trucking Assns., Inc.* (2001) ("Congress ... does not, one might say, hide elephants in mouseholes"). Put somewhat more directly, we would expect to see some affirmative indication of intent if Congress actually meant to make structured dismissals a backdoor means to achieve the exact kind of nonconsensual priority-violating final distributions that the Code prohibits in Chapter 7 liquidations and Chapter 11 plans.

We can find nothing in the statute that evinces this intent. The Code gives a bankruptcy court the power to "dismiss" a Chapter 11 case. §1112(b). But the word "dismiss" itself says nothing about the power to make nonconsensual priority-violating distributions of estate value. Neither the word "structured," nor the word "conditions," nor anything else about distributing estate value to creditors pursuant to a dismissal appears in any relevant part of the Code.

Insofar as the dismissal sections of Chapter 11 foresee any transfer of assets, they seek a restoration of the prepetition financial status quo. See §349(b)(1) (dismissal ordinarily reinstates a variety of avoided transfers and voided liens); §349(b)(2) (dismissal ordinarily vacates certain types of bankruptcy orders); §349(b)(3) (dismissal ordinarily "revests the property of the estate in the entity in which such property was vested immediately before the commencement of the case"); see also H.R.Rep. No. 95–595 (1977) (dismissal's "basic purpose ... is to undo the bankruptcy case, as far as practicable, and to restore all property rights to the position in which they were found at the commencement of the case").

Section 349(b), we concede, also says that a bankruptcy judge may, "for cause, orde[r] otherwise." But, read in context, this provision appears designed to give courts the flexibility to "make the appropriate orders to protect rights acquired in reliance on the bankruptcy case." H.R.Rep. No. 95–595; cf., *e.g., Wiese v. Community Bank of Central Wis.* (7th Cir. 2009) (upholding, under §349(b), a Bankruptcy Court's decision not to reinstate a debtor's claim against a bank that gave up a lien in reliance on the claim being released in the debtor's reorganization plan). Nothing else in the Code authorizes a court ordering a dismissal to make general end-of-case distributions of estate assets to creditors of the kind that normally take place in a Chapter 7 liquidation or Chapter 11 plan—let alone final distributions that do not help to restore the *status quo ante* or protect reliance interests acquired in the bankruptcy, and that would be flatly impermissible in a Chapter 7 liquidation or a Chapter 11 plan because they violate priority without the impaired creditors' consent. That being so, the word "cause" is too weak a reed upon which to rest so weighty a power. See *United Sav. Assn. of Tex. v. Timbers of Inwood Forest Associates, Ltd.* (1988) (noting that "[s]tatutory construction ... is a holistic endeavor" and that a court should select a "meanin[g that] produces a substantive effect that is compatible with the rest of the law"); *Kelly v. Robinson* (US 1986) (in interpreting a statute, a court "must not be guided by a single sentence or member of a sentence, but look to the provisions of the whole law, and to its object and policy" (internal quotation marks omitted)); cf. *In re Sadler* (7th Cir. 1991) ("'Cause' under §349(b) means an acceptable reason. Desire to make an end run around a statute is not an adequate reason").

We have found no contrary precedent, either from this Court, or, for that matter, from lower court decisions reflecting common bankruptcy practice. The Third Circuit referred briefly to *In re Buffet Partners, L.P.* (Bankr. N.D. Tex. 2014). The court in that case approved a structured dismissal. (We express no view about the legality of structured dismissals in general.) But at the same time it pointed out "that not one party with an economic stake in the case has objected to the dismissal in this manner."

The Third Circuit also relied upon *In re Iridium Operating LLC* (2d Cir. 2007). But *Iridium* did not involve a structured dismissal. It addressed an *interim* distribution of settlement proceeds to fund a litigation trust that would press claims on the estate's behalf. The *Iridium* court observed that, when evaluating this type of preplan settlement, "[i]t is difficult to employ the rule of priorities" because "the nature and extent of the Estate and the claims against it are *not yet fully resolved.*" *Id.,* at 464 (emphasis added). The decision does not state or suggest that the Code authorizes nonconsensual departures from ordinary priority rules in the context of a dismissal—which is a *final* distribution of estate value—and in the absence of any further unresolved bankruptcy issues.

We recognize that *Iridium* is not the only case in which a court has approved interim distributions that violate ordinary priority rules. But in such instances one can generally find significant Code-related objectives that the priority-violating distributions serve. Courts, for example, have approved "first-day" wage orders that allow payment of employees' prepetition wages, "critical vendor" orders that allow payment of essential suppliers' prepetition invoices, and "roll-ups" that allow lenders who continue financing the debtor to be paid first on their prepetition claims. See *Cybergenics*; D. Baird, *Elements of Bankruptcy* 232–234 (6th ed. 2014); Roe, 99 Va. L. Rev., at 1250–1264. In doing so, these courts have usually found that the distributions at issue would "enable a successful reorganization and make even the disfavored creditors better off." *In re Kmart Corp.* (7th Cir. 2004) (discussing the justifications for critical-vendor orders); see also *Toibb v. Radloff* (1991) (recognizing "permitting business debtors to reorganize and restructure their debts in order to revive the debtors' businesses" and "maximizing the value of the bankruptcy estate" as purposes of the Code). By way of contrast, in a structured dismissal like the one ordered below, the priority-violating distribution is attached to a final disposition; it does not preserve the debtor as a going concern; it does not make the disfavored creditors better off; it does not promote the possibility of a confirmable plan; it does not help to restore the *status quo ante*; and it does not protect reliance interests. In short, we cannot find in the violation of ordinary priority rules that occurred here any significant offsetting bankruptcy-related justification.

Rather, the distributions at issue here more closely resemble proposed transactions that lower courts have refused to allow on the ground that they circumvent the Code's procedural safeguards. See, *e.g., In re Braniff Airways, Inc.* (5th Cir. 1983) (prohibiting an attempt to "short circuit the requirements of Chapter 11 for confirmation of a reorganization plan by establishing the terms of the plan *sub rosa* in connection with a sale of assets"); *In re Lionel Corp.* (5th Cir. 1983) (reversing a Bankruptcy Court's approval of an asset sale after holding that §363 does not "gran[t] the bankruptcy judge *carte blanche*" or "swallo[w] up Chapter 11's safeguards"); *In re Biolitec, Inc.* (Bankr. N.J. 2014) (rejecting a structured dismissal because it "seeks to alter parties' rights without their consent and lacks many of the Code's most important safeguards"); cf. *In re Chrysler LLC* (2d Cir. 2009) (approving a §363 asset sale because the bankruptcy court demonstrated "proper solicitude for the priority between creditors and deemed it essential that the [s]ale in no way upset that priority"), *vacated as moot*, 592 F.3d 370 (2d Cir. 2010) (*per curiam*).

IV

We recognize that the Third Circuit did not approve nonconsensual priority-violating structured dismissals in general. To the contrary, the court held that they were permissible only in those "rare case[s]" in which courts could find "sufficient reasons" to disregard priority. Despite the "rare case" limitation, we still cannot agree.

For one thing, it is difficult to give precise content to the concept "sufficient reasons." That fact threatens to turn a "rare case" exception into a more general rule. Consider the present case. The Bankruptcy Court feared that (1) without the worker-skipping distribution, there would be no settlement, (2) without a settlement, all the unsecured creditors would receive nothing, and consequently (3) its distributions would make some creditors (high- and low-priority creditors) better off without making other (mid-priority) creditors worse off (for they would receive nothing regardless). But, as we have pointed out, the record provides equivocal support for the first two propositions. And, one can readily imagine other cases that turn on comparably dubious predictions. The result is uncertainty. And uncertainty will lead to similar claims being made in many, not just a few, cases. See Rudzik, *A Priority Is a Priority Is a Priority—Except When It Isn't*, 34 Am. Bankr. Inst. J. 16, 79 (2015) ("[O]nce the floodgates are opened, debtors and favored creditors can be expected to make every case that 'rare case'").

The consequences are potentially serious. They include departure from the protections Congress granted particular classes of creditors. See, *e.g., United States v. Embassy Restaurant, Inc.* (US 1959) (Congress established employee wage priority "to alleviate in some degree the hardship that unemployment usually brings to workers and their families" when an employer files for bankruptcy); H.R.Rep. No. 95–595 (explaining the importance of ensuring that employees do not "abandon a failing business for fear of not being paid"). They include changes in the bargaining power of different classes of creditors even in bankruptcies that do not end in structured dismissals. See Warren, *A Theory of Absolute Priority*, 1991 Ann. Survey Am. L. 9, 30. They include risks of collusion, *i.e.,* senior secured creditors and general unsecured creditors teaming up to squeeze out priority unsecured creditors. See *Bank of America Nat. Trust and Sav. Assn. v. 203 North LaSalle Street Partnership* (1999) (discussing how the absolute priority rule was developed in response to "concern with 'the ability of a few insiders, whether representatives of management or major creditors, to use the reorganization process to gain an unfair advantage'" (quoting H.R. Doc. No. 93–137 (1973))). And they include making settlement more difficult to achieve. See Landes & Posner, *Legal Precedent: A Theoretical and Empirical Analysis*, 19 J. Law & Econ. 249, 271 (1976) (arguing that "the ratio of lawsuits to settlements is mainly a function of the amount of uncertainty, which leads to divergent estimates by the parties of the probable outcome"); see also *RadLAX Gateway Hotel, LLC v. Amalgamated Bank* (2012) (noting the importance of clarity and predictability in light of the fact that the "Bankruptcy Code standardizes an expansive (and sometimes unruly) area of law").

For these reasons, as well as those set forth in Part III, we conclude that Congress did not authorize a "rare case" exception. We cannot "alter the balance struck by the statute," *Law v. Siegel* (US 2014), not even in "rare cases." Cf. *Norwest Bank Worthington v. Ahlers* (US 1988) (explaining that courts cannot deviate from the procedures "specified by the Code," even when they sincerely "believ[e] that … creditors would be better off"). The judgment of the Court of Appeals is reversed, and the case is remanded for further proceedings consistent with this opinion.

It is so ordered.

Justice THOMAS, with whom Justice ALITO joins, dissenting.

[The dissenters would have dismissed the writ of *certiorari* as improvidently granted on the ground that the petition failed to properly raise the structured dismissal question addressed by the Court].

NOTE

An early, post-*Jevic* decision rejecting a priority deviating settlement is *In re Fryar*, 570 B.R. 602 (Bankr. E.D. Tenn. 2017). *Fryar* began the difficult line-drawing task between an interim order (in which the Supreme Court appears to be open to some level of priority deviation if appropriately justified) and a forbidden priority-deviating final disposition. In *Fryar* the court found the "interim" settlement to be a prelude to an inevitable conversion or dismissal of the case and found the priority deviation impermissible on that basis.

4.   NEW VALUE RULE

E. THE FUTURE OF CHAPTER 11 REORGANIZATIONS

F. EFFECT OF CONFIRMATION OF PLAN

G. MODIFICATION OF PLAN

CHAPTER 12

THE SALE ALTERNATIVE UNDER SECTION 363

A. INTRODUCTION

B. SALE OR LEASE OF PROPERTY IN THE ORDINARY COURSE

C. GOING CONCERN SALES UNDER SECTION 363

D. SELLING FREE AND CLEAR UNDER SECTION 363(f)

1. LIENS

> Append to Note 3 following *In re PW*, at p. 732:

Although courts have traditionally viewed §363(m) as embodying a statutory mootness principle, the Seventh Circuit takes the position that §363(m) does not make an appeal moot, but rather constitutes a statutory defense to an action to upset a sale on appeal. *Trinity 83 Development v. ColFin Midwest Funding*, 917 F.3d 599 (7th Cir. 2019). It is unclear whether viewing §363(m) in this way makes a significant procedural or substantive difference. Presumably, the 363(m) "defense" is not available at the bankruptcy court level and may continue to be raised for the first time on appeal by motion under Federal Rule of Appellate Procedure 27 or Federal Rule of Bankruptcy Procedure 8013, or in merits briefing on appeal. The Seventh Circuit's view that §363(m) is a personal affirmative defense of the buyer or lessee implies that other parties to the sale order (for example creditors claiming an interest in sale proceeds) may not obtain 363(m) protection. *Id.* But unlike *PW*, *Trinity 83* does not appear to undercut the free and clear buyer's protection under §363(f). Most courts applying the statutory mootness concept have adopted a similar view of the scope of §363(m), protecting buyers from creditors and other parties claiming through the estate, but not precluding review of the distribution of sale proceeds among creditors.

2. SUCCESSOR LIABILITY

> Following *In re Trans World Airlines*, p. 744, insert:

Matter of Motors Liquidation Co.

United States Court of Appeals, Second Circuit, 2016.
829 F.3d 135, *cert. denied*, 137 S.Ct. 1813.

■ CHIN, Circuit Judge:

On June 1, 2009, General Motors Corporation ("Old GM"), the nation's largest manufacturer of automobiles and the creator of such iconic American brands as Chevrolet and Cadillac, filed for bankruptcy. During the financial crisis of 2007 and 2008, as access to credit tightened and consumer spending diminished, Old GM posted net losses of $70 billion over the course of a year and a half. The U.S. Department of the Treasury ("Treasury") loaned billions of dollars from the Troubled Asset Relief Program ("TARP") to buy the company time to revamp its business model. When Old GM's private efforts failed, President Barack Obama announced to the nation a solution—"a quick, surgical bankruptcy." Old GM petitioned for Chapter 11 bankruptcy protection, and only forty days later the new General Motors LLC ("New GM") emerged.

This case involves one of the consequences of the GM bankruptcy. Beginning in February 2014, New GM began recalling cars due to a defect in their ignition switches. The defect was potentially lethal: while in motion, a car's ignition could accidentally turn off, shutting down the engine, disabling power steering and braking, and deactivating the airbags.

Many of the cars in question were built years before the GM bankruptcy, but individuals claiming harm from the ignition switch defect faced a potential barrier created by the bankruptcy process. In bankruptcy, Old GM had used 11 U.S.C. §363 of the Bankruptcy Code (the "Code") to sell its assets to New GM "free and clear." In plain terms, where individuals might have had claims against Old GM, a "free and clear" provision in the bankruptcy court's sale order (the "Sale Order") barred those same claims from being brought against New GM as the successor corporation.

Various individuals nonetheless initiated class action lawsuits against New GM, asserting "successor liability" claims and seeking damages for losses and injuries arising from the ignition switch defect and other defects. New GM argued that, because of the "free and clear" provision, claims could only be brought against Old GM, and not New GM.

On April 15, 2015, the United States Bankruptcy Court for the Southern District of New York (Gerber, *J.*) agreed and enforced the Sale Order to enjoin many of these claims against New GM. Though the bankruptcy court also determined that these plaintiffs did not have notice of the Sale Order as required by the Due Process Clause of the Fifth Amendment, the bankruptcy court denied plaintiffs relief from the Sale Order on all but a subset of claims. ...

We affirm, reverse, and vacate in part the bankruptcy court's decision to enforce the Sale Order against plaintiffs....

BACKGROUND

I. Bailout

In the final two quarters of 2007, as the American economy suffered a significant downturn, Old GM posted net losses of approximately $39 billion and $722 million. General Motors Corp., *Annual Report (Form 10–K)* 245 (Mar. 5, 2009). In 2008, it posted quarterly net losses of approximately $3.3 billion, $15.5 billion, $2.5 billion, and $9.6 billion. *Id.* In a year and a half, Old GM had managed to hemorrhage over $70 billion.

The possibility of Old GM's collapse alarmed many. Old GM employed roughly 240,000 workers and provided pensions to another 500,000 retirees. The company also purchased parts from over eleven thousand suppliers and marketed through roughly six thousand dealerships. A disorderly collapse of Old GM would have far-reaching consequences.

After Congress declined to bail out Old GM, President George W. Bush announced on December 19, 2008 that the executive branch would provide emergency loans to help automakers "stave off bankruptcy while they develop plans for viability." In Old GM's case, TARP loaned $13.4 billion on the condition that Old GM both submit a business plan for long-term viability to the President no later than February 17, 2009 and undergo any necessary revisions no later than March 31, 2009. If the President found the business plan unsatisfactory, the TARP funds would become due and payable in thirty days, rendering Old GM insolvent and effectively forcing it into bankruptcy.

On March 30, 2009, President Obama told the nation that Old GM's business plan was not viable. At the same time, the President provided Old GM with another $6 billion loan and sixty more days to revise its plan along certain parameters. President Obama also reassured the public:

> But just in case there's still nagging doubts, let me say it as plainly as I can: If you buy a car from Chrysler or General Motors, you will be able to get your car serviced and repaired, just like always. Your warranty will be safe. In fact, it will be safer than it's ever been, because starting today, the United States Government will stand behind your warranty.

As the President stood behind the reliability of GM cars, pledging another $600 million to back all warranty coverage, bankruptcy remained a stark possibility.

II. Bankruptcy

The federal aid did not succeed in averting bankruptcy. Old GM fared no better in the first quarter of 2009—posting on May 8, 2009 a $5.9 billion net loss. General Motors Corp., *Quarterly Report (Form 10–Q)* 57 (May 8, 2009). But entering bankruptcy posed a unique set of problems: Old GM sought to restructure and become profitable again, not to shut down; yet if Old GM lingered in bankruptcy too long, operating expenses would accumulate and consumer confidence in the GM brand could deteriorate, leaving Old GM no alternative but to liquidate and close once and for all. On June 1, 2009, with these risks in mind, Old GM petitioned for Chapter 11 bankruptcy protection in the United States Bankruptcy Court for the Southern District of New York.

A. Mechanics of the §363 Sale

The same day, Old GM filed a motion to sell itself to New GM (also dubbed "Vehicle Acquisition Holdings LLC" or "NGMCO, Inc."), complete with a 103-page draft sale agreement and 30-page proposed sale order.

Through this proposed sale, Old GM was attempting not a traditional Chapter 11 reorganization, but a transaction pursuant to §363—a less common way of effecting a bankruptcy. The usual Chapter 11 reorganization follows set procedures: the company entering bankruptcy (the "debtor") files a reorganization plan disclosing to creditors how they will be treated, asks those creditors to vote to accept the plan, and then emerges from bankruptcy with its liabilities restructured along certain parameters. This jostling can take years. In contrast in a §363 sale of substantially all assets, the debtor does not truly "reorganize." Instead, it sells its primary assets to a successor corporation, which immediately takes over the business. As evidenced by the GM bankruptcy, a §363 sale can close in a matter of weeks.

The proposed sale was, in effect, a complex transaction made possible by bankruptcy law. GM's sale would proceed in several parts. First, Old GM would become a "debtor-in-possession" under the Code. Where a trustee might otherwise be appointed to assert outside control of the debtor, a debtor-in-possession continues operating its business. Still in control, Old GM could seek the bankruptcy court's permission to sell portions of its business. *See* §363(b)(1).

Second, there would be New GM, a company owned predominantly by Treasury (over sixty percent). As proposed, New GM would acquire from Old GM substantially all of its business—what one might commonly think of as the automaker "GM." But New GM would not take on all of Old GM's liabilities. The Code allows a §363 sale "free and clear of any interest in such property." §363(f). The proposed sale order provided that New GM would acquire Old GM assets "free and clear of all liens, claims, encumbrances, and other interests of any kind or nature whatsoever, including rights or claims based on any successor or transferee liability." Other than a few liabilities that New GM would assume as its own, this "free and clear" provision would act as a liability shield to prevent individuals with claims against Old GM from suing New GM. Once the sale closed, the "bankruptcy" would be done: New GM could immediately begin operating the GM business, free of Old GM's debts.

Third, Old GM would remain. The proposed sale would leave Old GM with some assets, including $1.175 billion in cash, interests in the Saturn brand, and certain real and personal property. Old GM would also receive consideration from New GM, including a promise to repay Treasury and Canadian government loans used to finance the business through bankruptcy and a ten-percent equity stake in New GM. Old GM would retain, however, the bulk of its old liabilities.

Fourth, Old GM would liquidate. Though liquidation is not formally part of a §363 sale, the sale would result in two GM companies. Old GM would disband: it would rename itself "Motors Liquidation Company" and arrange a plan for liquidation that addressed how its remaining liabilities would be paid. *See* §1129(a)(11). Thus, while New GM would quickly emerge from bankruptcy to operate the GM business, Old GM would remain in bankruptcy and undergo a traditional, lengthy liquidation process.

B. Sale Order

One day after Old GM filed its motion, on June 2, 2009, the bankruptcy court ordered Old GM to provide notice of the proposed sale order. Old GM was required to send direct mail notice of its proposed sale order to numerous interested parties, including "all parties who are known to have asserted any lien, claim, encumbrance, or interest in or on [the to-be-sold assets]," and to post publication notice of the same in major publications, including the *Wall Street Journal* and *New York Times.* The sale notice specified that interested parties would have until June 19, 2009 to submit to the bankruptcy court responses and objections to the proposed sale order.

The bankruptcy court proceeded to hear over 850 objections to the proposed sale order over the course of three days, between June 30 and July 2, 2009. On July 5, 2009, after addressing and dismissing the objections, the bankruptcy court approved the §363 sale. Among those objections were arguments against the imposition of a "free and clear" provision to bar claims against New GM as the successor to Old GM made by consumer organizations, state attorneys general, and accident victims.

Next, the bankruptcy court issued the Sale Order, which entered into effect the final sale agreement between Old GM and New GM (the "Sale Agreement"). In the Sale Agreement, New GM assumed fifteen categories of liabilities. As relevant here, New GM agreed to assume liability for accidents *after* the closing date for the §363 sale and to make repairs pursuant to express warranties issued in connection with the sale of GM cars—two liability provisions present in the initial draft sale agreement. The Sale Agreement also provided a new provision—resulting from negotiations among state attorneys general, the GM parties, and Treasury during the course of the sale hearing—that New GM would assume liability for any Lemon Law claims. With these exceptions, New GM would be "free and clear" of any and all liabilities of Old GM.

On July 10, 2009, the §363 sale officially closed, and New GM began operating the automaker business. As a matter of public perception, the GM bankruptcy was over—the company had exited bankruptcy in forty days.

C. Liquidation of Old GM

Meanwhile, Old GM remained in bankruptcy. Over the next several years, the bankruptcy court managed the process of satisfying liabilities that remained with Old GM (*i.e.*, not taken on by New GM).

The bankruptcy court set November 30, 2009 as the "bar date" for any individual or entity to file a proof of claim—that is, to assert a claim as to Old GM's remaining assets. Old GM filed its first Chapter 11 liquidation plan on August 31, 2010, and amended it on December 8, 2010 and again on March 29, 2011. The proposed plan provided how claims against Old GM would be paid: secured claims, other priority claims, and environmental claims made by the government would be paid in full; unsecured claims (claims without an assurance of payment, such as in the form of a lien on property) would not.

Instead, under the plan, Old GM would establish GUC Trust, which would be administered by the Wilmington Trust Company. Once GUC Trust (and other like trusts) was established, Old GM would dissolve.

GUC Trust would hold certain Old GM assets—including New GM stock and stock warrants that could be used to purchase shares at fixed prices, along with other financial instruments. Creditors with unsecured claims against Old GM would receive these New GM securities and "units" of GUC Trust (the value of which would be pegged to the residual value of GUC Trust) on a pro rata basis in satisfaction of their claims. The Sale Agreement also imposed an "accordion feature" to ensure that GUC Trust would remain adequately funded in the event that the amount of unsecured claims grew too large. The accordion feature provided that if "the Bankruptcy Court makes a finding that the estimated aggregate allowed general unsecured claims against [Old GM's] estates exceed $35 [billion], then [New GM] will ... issue 10,000,000 additional shares of Common Stock ... to [Old GM]."

On March 29, 2011, the bankruptcy court confirmed this liquidation plan. GUC Trust made quarterly distributions of its assets thereafter. The initial distribution released more than seventy-five percent of the New GM securities.

On February 8, 2012, the bankruptcy court ordered that no further claims against Old GM and payable by GUC Trust would be allowed unless the claim amended a prior claim, was filed with GUC Trust's consent, or was deemed timely filed by the bankruptcy court. As of March 31, 2014, GUC Trust had distributed roughly ninety percent of its New GM securities and nearly 32 million units of GUC Trust; the expected value of unsecured claims against Old GM totaled roughly $32 billion, not enough to trigger the accordion feature and involve New GM in the bankruptcy. The GM bankruptcy that began five years earlier appeared to be approaching its end.

III. Ignition Switch Defect

On February 7, 2014, New GM first informed the National Highway Traffic Safety Administration ("NHTSA") that it would be recalling, among other vehicles, the 2005 Chevrolet Cobalt. A defect in the ignition switch could prevent airbags from deploying.

A later congressional staff report, which followed four days of testimony by New GM CEO Mary Barra before committees of the House of Representatives and Senate, described what could happen by referring to an actual tragic accident caused by the defect: In October 2006, three teenagers were riding in a 2005 Chevrolet Cobalt when the driver lost control and the car careened off the side of the road. The vehicle flew into a telephone utility box and several trees. The airbags did not deploy, and two of the teenagers died.

From February until October 2014, New GM would issue over 60 recalls, with the number of affected vehicles in the United States alone surpassing 25 million. New GM hired attorney Anton Valukas of the law firm Jenner & Block to investigate; he did so and prepared an extensive report (the "Valukas Report").

In 1997, Old GM sold three out of ten cars on the road in North America. Engineers began developing a new ignition switch that could be used in multiple vehicles across the GM brand, first by setting technical specifications for the switch and then by testing prototypes against those specifications.

Throughout testing, which lasted until 2002, prototypes consistently failed to meet technical specifications. In particular, a low amount of torque could cause the ignition switch to switch to "accessory" or "off." A low torque threshold on an ignition switch would mean that little force—perhaps even the bump of a stray knee—would be needed to rotate the key in the switch from the "on" position to the "accessory" or "off" position.

Near the end of testing, an engineer commented on the ignition switch's lingering problems in an email: he was "tired of the switch from hell." Three months later, in May 2002, the ignition switch was approved for production, despite never having passed testing.

In the fall of 2002, Old GM began producing vehicles with the faulty ignition switch. Almost immediately, customers complained of moving stalls, sometimes at highway speeds—instances where the engine and power steering and braking cut off while the car was in motion, leaving drivers to manually maneuver the vehicle, that is, without assistance of the car's power steering and braking systems.

Despite customer complaints, and grumblings in the press, Old GM classified the moving stall as a "non-safety issue." As Valukas put it, "on a scale of 1 (most severe) to 4 (least severe) … the problem could have been designated a severity level 1 safety problem, [but] it was not." Instead, the moving stall was assigned a severity level of 3. Old GM personnel considered the problem to be a matter of customer satisfaction, not safety. These personnel apparently also did not then fully realize that when a car shuts off, so do its airbags. But as early as August 2001, at least some Old GM engineers understood that turning off the ignition switch could prevent airbags from deploying.

Complaints about the ignition switch continued. Between 2004 and 2005, NHTSA began asking questions about engine stalls. In 2005, several media outlets also reported on the stalls. *See, e.g.*, Jeff Sabatini, *Making a Case for Keyless Ignitions*, N.Y. Times (June 19, 2005). Senior attorneys studied the stalls, but considered the risk to be "remote[ ]." At the same time, Old GM's product investigations unit recreated the ignition switch's issues by using only a heavy keychain to generate torque. Finally, in December 2005, Old GM issued a bulletin to dealers, but not to customers, warning them that "low ignition key cylinder torque" could cause cars to turn off. The bulletin did not mention that, as a result, cars could stall on the road.

Then came reports of fatalities. In late 2005 through 2006, news of deaths from airbag non-deployments in crashes where airbags should have deployed reached the desks of Old GM's legal team. Around April 2006, Old GM engineers decided on a design change of the ignition switch to increase the torque. Old GM engineers did so quietly, without changing the ignition switch's part number, a change that would have signaled that improvements or adjustments had been made.

In February 2007, a Wisconsin state trooper's report made its way into the files of Old GM's legal department: "The two front seat airbags did not deploy. It appears that the ignition switch had somehow been turned from the run position to accessory prior to the collision with the trees." NHTSA similarly brought to Old GM's attention reported airbag non-deployments. *See* Transportation Research Center, Indiana University, *On-Site Air Bag Non-Deployment Investigation 7* (Apr. 25, 2007, rev. Mar. 31, 2008). As more incidents with its cars piled up, Old GM finally drafted an updated bulletin to dealers warning them of possible "stalls," but never sent it out.

Old GM internally continued to investigate. By May 2009, staff had figured out that non-deployment of airbags in these crashes was attributable to a sudden loss of power. They believed that one of the two "most likely explanation[s] for the power mode signal change was … a problem with the Ignition Switch." By June 2009, Old GM engineers had implemented a change to the ignition key, hoping to fix the problem once and for all. One engineer lamented that "[t]his issue has been around since man first lumbered out of [the] sea and stood on two feet."

Later, the Valukas Report commented on the general attitude at Old GM. For eleven years, "GM heard over and over from various quarters—including customers, dealers, the press, and their own employees—that the car's ignition switch led to moving stalls, group after group and committee after committee within GM that reviewed the issue failed to take action or acted too slowly.

Although everyone had responsibility to fix the problem, nobody took responsibility."

The Valukas Report recounted aspects of GM's corporate culture. With the "GM salute," employees would attend action meetings and literally cross their arms and point fingers at others to shirk responsibility. With the "GM nod," employees would (again) literally nod in agreement to endorse a proposed plan, understanding that they and others had no intention of following through. Finally, the Report described how GM employees, instead of taking action, would claim the need to keep searching for the "root cause" of the moving stalls and airbag non-deployments. This "search for root cause became a basis for doing nothing to resolve the problem for years."

Indeed, New GM would not begin recalling cars for ignition switch defects until February 2014. Soon after New GM's initial recall, individuals filed dozens of class actions lawsuits, claiming that the ignition switch defect caused personal injuries and economic losses, both before and after the §363 sale closed. New GM sought to enforce the Sale Order, invoking the liability shield to hold New GM "free and clear" of various claims. This meant that when it came to Old GM cars New GM would pay for post-closing personal injuries, make repairs, and follow Lemon Laws, but nothing else. The amount of purportedly barred liabilities was substantial—an estimated $7 to $10 billion in economic losses, not to mention damages from pre-closing accidents.

IV. Proceedings Below

On April 21, 2014, Steven Groman and others (the "Groman Plaintiffs") initiated an adversary proceeding against New GM in the bankruptcy court below, asserting economic losses arising from the ignition switch defect. The same day, New GM moved to enforce the Sale Order to enjoin those claims, as well as claims in other ignition switch actions then being pursued against New GM.

Other plaintiffs allegedly affected by the Sale Order included classes of individuals who had suffered pre-closing injuries arising from the ignition switch defect ("Pre-Closing Accident Plaintiffs"), economic losses arising from the ignition switch defect in Old GM cars ("Ignition Switch Plaintiffs"), and damages arising from defects other than the ignition switch in Old GM cars ("Non-Ignition Switch Plaintiffs"). Included within the Ignition Switch Plaintiffs were individuals who had purchased Old GM cars secondhand after the §363 sale closed ("Used Car Purchasers").

On appeal, several orders are before us. First, the Non-Ignition Switch Plaintiffs filed a motion, asserting, among other things, that the bankruptcy court lacked jurisdiction to enforce the Sale Order. On August 6, 2014, the bankruptcy court denied that motion.

Second, after receiving further briefing and hearing oral argument on the motion to enforce, on April 15, 2015 the bankruptcy court decided to enforce the Sale Order in part and dismiss any would-be claims against GUC Trust because relief would be equitably moot. The bankruptcy court first determined plaintiffs lacked notice consistent with procedural due process. In particular, the bankruptcy court found that the ignition switch claims were known to or reasonably ascertainable by Old GM prior to the sale, and thus plaintiffs were entitled to actual notice, as opposed to the mere publication notice that they received. The bankruptcy court found, however, that with one exception plaintiffs had not been "prejudiced" by this lack of notice—the exception being claims stemming from New GM's own wrongful conduct in concealing defects (so-called "independent claims"). In other words, the bankruptcy court held that New GM could not be sued—in bankruptcy court or elsewhere—for ignition switch claims that otherwise could have been brought against Old GM, unless those claims arose from New GM's own wrongful conduct.

...

DISCUSSION

The Code permits a debtor to sell substantially all of its assets to a successor corporation through a §363 sale, outside of the normal reorganization process. Here, no party seeks to undo the sale of Old GM's assets to New GM, as executed through the Sale Order. Instead, plaintiffs challenge the extent to which the bankruptcy court may absolve New GM, as a successor corporation, of Old GM's liabilities. *See generally* 3 *Collier on Bankruptcy* ¶ 363.02 (noting that "use of a section 363 sale probably reached its zenith" with the GM bankruptcy). In particular, they dispute whether New GM may use the Sale Order's "free and clear" provision to shield itself from claims primarily arising out of the ignition switch defect and other defects.

I. Jurisdiction

...

II. Scope of "Free and Clear" Provision

We turn to the scope of the Sale Order. The Sale Order transferred assets from Old GM to New GM "free and clear of liens, claims, encumbrances, and other interests ..., including rights or claims ... based on any successor or transferee liability." The bankruptcy court did not explicitly address what claims were covered by the Sale Order.

We address the scope of the Sale Order because it implicates our procedural due process analysis that follows. If the Sale Order covers certain claims, then we would have to consider whether plaintiffs' due process rights are violated by applying the "free and clear" clause to those claims. If the Sale Order did not cover certain claims, however, then those claims could not be enjoined by enforcing the Sale Order and due process concerns would not be implicated. We interpret the Sale Order *de novo* to determine what claims are barred.

A. Applicable Law

The Code allows the trustee or debtor-in-possession to "use, sell, or lease, other than in the ordinary course of business, property of the estate." §363(b)(1). A sale pursuant to §363(b) may be made "free and clear of any interest in such property" if any condition on a list of conditions is met. §363(f). "Yet the Code does not define the concept of 'interest,' of which the property may be sold free and clear," 3 *Collier on Bankruptcy* ¶ 363.06, nor does it express the extent to which "claims" fall within the ambit of "interests."

New GM asserts that *In re Chrysler LLC* (2d Cir. 2009), resolved that successor liability claims are interests. But *Chrysler* was vacated by the Supreme Court after it became moot during the *certiorari* process and remanded with instructions to dismiss the appeal as moot. We had not addressed the issue before *Chrysler*, and now that case is no longer controlling precedent.

Rather than formulating a single precise definition for "any interest in such property," courts have continued to address the phrase "on a case-by-case basis." At minimum, the language in §363(f) permits the sale of property free and clear of *in rem* interests in the property, such as liens that attach to the property. *See In re Trans World Airlines, Inc.* (3d Cir. 2003). But courts have permitted a "broader definition that encompasses other obligations that may flow from ownership of the property." 3 *Collier on Bankruptcy* ¶ 363.06. Sister courts have held that §363(f) may be used to bar a variety of successor liability claims that relate to ownership of property: an "interest" might encompass Coal Act obligations otherwise placed upon a successor purchasing coal assets, *In re Leckie Smokeless Coal Co.* (4th Cir. 1996), travel vouchers issued to settle an airline's discrimination claims in a sale of airline assets, *Trans World Airlines*, or a license for future use of intellectual property when that property is sold, *FutureSource LLC v. Reuters Ltd.* (7th Cir. 2002). *See generally Precision Indus., Inc. v. Qualitech Steel SBQ* (7th Cir. 2003) ("[T]he term 'interest' is a broad term no doubt selected by Congress to avoid 'rigid and technical definitions drawn from other areas of the law.'"). In these instances, courts require "a relationship between the[ ] right to demand ... payments from the debtors and the use to which the debtors had put their assets." *Trans World Airlines*.

We agree that successor liability claims can be "interests" when they flow from a debtor's ownership of transferred assets. *See* 3 *Collier in Bankruptcy* ¶¶ 363.06; *Trans World Airlines*. But successor liability claims must also still qualify as "claims" under Chapter 11. Though §363(f) does not expressly invoke the Chapter 11 definition of "claims," *see* 11 U.S.C. §101(5), it makes sense to "harmonize" Chapter 11 reorganizations and §363 sales "to the extent permitted by the statutory language." *Chrysler*; *see Lionel* ("[S]ome play for the operation of both §363(b) and Chapter 11 must be allowed for."). Here, the bankruptcy court's power to bar "claims" in a quick §363 sale is plainly no broader than its power in a traditional Chapter 11 reorganization. *Compare* 11 U.S.C. §363(f) ("free and clear of any interest in such property"), *with* §1141(c) ("free and clear of all claims and interests"). We thus consider what claims may be barred under Chapter 11 generally.

Section 101(5) defines "claim" as any "right to payment, whether or not such right is reduced to judgment, liquidated, unliquidated, fixed, contingent, matured, unmatured, disputed, undisputed, legal, equitable, secured, or unsecured." A claim is (1) a right to payment (2) that arose before the filing of the petition. If the right to payment is contingent on future events, the claim must instead "result from pre-petition conduct fairly giving rise to that contingent claim." *In re Chateaugay Corp.* ("*Chateaugay I*") (2d Cir. 1991).

This Court has not decided, however, "the difficult case of pre-petition conduct that has not yet resulted in detectable injury, much less the extreme case of pre-petition conduct that has not yet resulted in any tortious consequence to a victim." *Chateaugay I* considered a hypothetical bankrupt bridge building company, which could predict that out of the 10,000 bridges it built, one would one day fail, causing deaths and other injuries. If that bridge did fail, the individuals might have tort claims resulting from pre-petition conduct, namely the building of the bridge.

Recognizing these claims would engender "enormous practical and perhaps constitutional problems." *Id.* Thus, "'claim' cannot be extended to include ... claimants whom the record indicates were completely unknown and unidentified at the time [the debtor] filed its petition and whose rights depended entirely on the fortuity of future occurrences." *Lemelle v. Universal Mfg. Corp.* (5th Cir. 1994). To avoid any practical and constitutional problems, courts require some minimum "contact," *Chateaugay I*, or "relationship," *Chateaugay*

IV, that makes identifiable the individual with whom the claim does or would rest.

To summarize, a bankruptcy court may approve a §363 sale "free and clear" of successor liability claims if those claims flow from the debtor's ownership of the sold assets. Such a claim must arise from a (1) right to payment (2) that arose before the filing of the petition or resulted from pre-petition conduct fairly giving rise to the claim. Further, there must be some contact or relationship between the debtor and the claimant such that the claimant is identifiable.

B. Application

We apply these principles to: (1) pre-closing accident claims, (2) economic loss claims arising from the ignition switch defect or other defects, (3) independent claims relating only to New GM's conduct, and (4) Used Car Purchasers' claims. The bankruptcy court assumed that the Sale Order's broad language suggested that all of these claims fell within the scope of the "free and clear" provision. We hold, however, that the first two sets of claims are covered by the Sale Order but that the latter two sets of claims are not.

First, the pre-closing accident claims clearly fall within the scope of the Sale Order. Those claims directly relate to the ownership of the GM automaker's business—Old GM built cars with ignition switch defects. And those plaintiffs' claims are properly thought of as tort claims that arose before the filing of the petition; indeed, the claims arise from accidents that occurred pre-closing involving Old GM cars.

Second, the economic loss claims arising from the ignition switch defect or other defects present a closer call. Like the claims of Pre-Closing Accident Plaintiffs, these claims flow from the operation of Old GM's automaker business. These individuals also, by virtue of owning Old GM cars, had come into contact with the debtor prior to the bankruptcy petition. Yet the ignition switch defect (and other defects) were only revealed some five years later.

GUC Trust thus asserts that there was no right to payment prior to the petition. We disagree. The economic losses claimed by these individuals were "contingent" claims. §101(5). That is, the ignition switch defect was there, but was not yet so patent that an individual could, as a practical matter, bring a case in court. The contingency standing in the way was Old GM telling plaintiffs that the ignition switch defect existed. In other words, Old GM's creation of the ignition switch defect fairly gave rise to these claims, even if the claimants did not yet know.

Third, however, the independent claims do not meet the Code's limitation on claims. By definition, independent claims are claims based on New GM's own post-closing wrongful conduct. Though the parties do not lay out the whole universe of possible independent claims, we can imagine that some claims involve misrepresentations by New GM as to the safety of Old GM cars. These sorts of claims are based on New GM's *post*-petition conduct, and are not claims that are based on a right to payment that arose before the filing of petition or that are based on pre-petition conduct. Thus, these claims are outside the scope of the Sale Order's "free and clear" provision.

Fourth, the Sale Order likewise does not cover the Used Car Purchasers' claims. The Used Car Purchasers were individuals who purchased Old GM cars *after* the closing, without knowledge of the defect or possible claim against New GM. They had no relation with Old GM prior to bankruptcy. Indeed, as of the bankruptcy petition there were an unknown number of unknown individuals who would one day purchase Old GM vehicles secondhand. There could have been no contact or relationship—actual or presumed—between Old GM and these specific plaintiffs, who otherwise had no awareness of the ignition switch defect or putative claims against New GM. We cannot, consistent with bankruptcy law, read the Sale Order to cover their claims.

New GM argues that "modifying" the Sale Order would "knock the props out of the foundation on which the [Sale Order] was based" or otherwise be unlawful. But we do not *modify* the Sale Order. Instead, we merely interpret the Sale Order in accordance with bankruptcy law. Indeed, by filing a motion to enforce, New GM in effect asked for the courts to interpret the Sale Order.

In sum, the "free and clear" provision covers pre-closing accident claims and economic loss claims based on the ignition switch and other defects. It does not cover independent claims or Used Car Purchasers' claims. Accordingly, we affirm the bankruptcy court's decision not to enjoin independent claims, and reverse its decision to enjoin the Used Car Purchasers' claims.

III. Procedural Due Process

The Sale Order covers the pre-closing accident claims and economic loss claims based on the ignition switch and other defects. The Sale Order, if enforced, would thus bar those claims. Plaintiffs contend on appeal that enforcing the Sale Order would violate procedural due process. We address two issues: (1) what notice plaintiffs were entitled to as a matter of procedural due process, and (2) if they were provided inadequate notice, whether the bankruptcy court erred in denying relief on the basis that most plaintiffs were not "prejudiced."

A. Notice

The bankruptcy court first concluded that plaintiffs were not provided notice as required by procedural due process. The bankruptcy court held that because Old GM knew or with reasonable diligence should have known of the ignition switch claims, plaintiffs were entitled to actual or direct mail notice, but received only publication notice. The parties dispute the extent of Old GM's knowledge of the ignition switch problem.

1. Applicable Law

The Due Process Clause provides, "No person shall ... be deprived of life, liberty, or property, without due process of law." U.S. Const. amend. V. Certain procedural protections attach when "deprivations trigger due process." Generally, legal claims are sufficient to constitute property such that a deprivation would trigger due process scrutiny.

Once due process is triggered, the question becomes what process is due. "An elementary and fundamental requirement of due process in any proceeding which is to be accorded finality is notice reasonably calculated, under all the circumstances, to apprise interested parties of the pendency of the action and afford them an opportunity to present their objections." *Mullane v. Cent. Hanover Bank & Tr. Co.* (US 1950). Courts ask "whether the state acted reasonably in selecting means likely to inform persons affected, not whether each property owner actually received notice." Notice is adequate if "[t]he means employed [are] such as one desirous of actually informing the absentee might reasonably adopt to accomplish it." *Mullane*.

This requirement also applies to bankruptcy proceedings. Indeed, a fundamental purpose of bankruptcy is to discharge, restructure, or impair claims against the debtor in an orderly fashion. "The general rule that emerges … is that notice by publication is not enough with respect to a person whose name and address are known or very easily ascertainable and whose legally protected interests are directly affected by the proceedings in question." *Schroeder v. City of New York* (US 1962). In other words, adequacy of notice "turns on what the debtor … knew about the claim or, with reasonable diligence, should have known." If the debtor knew or reasonably should have known about the claims, then due process entitles potential claimants to actual notice of the bankruptcy proceedings, but if the claims were unknown, publication notice suffices. *Chemetron* (3d Cir.1995).

If a debtor reveals in bankruptcy the claims against it and provides potential claimants notice consistent with due process of law, then the Code affords vast protections. Both §1141(c) and §363(f) permit "free and clear" provisions that act as liability shield. These provisions provide enormous incentives for a struggling company to be forthright. But if a debtor does not reveal claims that it is aware of, then bankruptcy law cannot protect it. Courts must "limit[ ] the opportunity for a completely unencumbered new beginning to the 'honest but unfortunate debtor.'" [*Local Loan v. Hunt*].

2. Application

The parties do not dispute that plaintiffs received only publication notice. The question is whether they were entitled to more. The bankruptcy court found that because Old GM knew or reasonably should have known about the ignition switch defect prior to bankruptcy, it should have provided direct mail notice to vehicle owners. We find no clear error in this factual finding.

As background, federal law requires that automakers keep records of the first owners of their vehicles. 49 U.S.C. §30117(b)(1) ("A manufacturer of a motor vehicle … shall cause to be maintained a record of the name and address of the first purchaser of each vehicle …."). This provision facilitates recalls and other consequences of the consumer-automaker relationship. Thus, to the extent that Old GM knew of defects in its cars, it would also necessarily know the identity of a significant number of affected owners.

The facts paint a picture that Old GM did nothing, even as it knew that the ignition switch defect impacted consumers. From its development in 1997, the ignition switch never passed Old GM's own technical specifications. Old GM knew that the switch was defective, but it approved the switch for millions of cars anyway.

Once the ignition switch was installed, Old GM almost immediately received various complaints. News outlets reported about the faulty ignition switch. NHTSA approached Old GM about moving stalls and airbag non-deployments. A police report, which Old GM's legal team possessed, linked these breakdowns to a faulty ignition switch. Old GM even considered warning dealers (but not consumers) about moving stalls. By May 2009, at the latest, Old GM personnel had essentially concluded that the ignition switch, moving stalls, and airbag non-deployments were related. Considering the airbag issues, they believed that one of the two "most likely explanation[s] for the power mode signal change was … a problem with the Ignition Switch."

A bankruptcy court could reasonably read from this record that Old GM knew about the ignition switch defect. Old GM knew that the defect caused stalls and had linked the airbag non-deployments to the defect by May 2009.

Even assuming the bankruptcy court erred in concluding that Old GM *knew*, Old GM—if reasonably diligent—surely *should have known* about the defect. Old GM engineers should have followed up when they learned their ignition switch did not initially pass certain technical specifications. Old GM lawyers should have followed up when they heard disturbing reports about airbag non-deployments or moving stalls. Old GM product safety teams should have followed up when they were able to recreate the ignition switch defect with ease after being approached by NHTSA. If any of these leads had been diligently pursued in the seven years between 2002 and 2009, Old GM likely would have learned that the ignition switch defect posed a hazard for vehicle owners.

Such "reckless disregard of the facts [is] sufficient to satisfy the requirement of knowledge." In the face of all the reports and complaints of faulty ignition switches, moving stalls, airbag non-deployments, and, indeed, serious accidents, and in light of the conclusions of its own personnel, Old GM had an obligation to take steps to "acquire full or exact knowledge of the nature and extent" of the defect. Under these circumstances, Old GM had a duty to identify the cause of the problem and fix it. Instead, the Valukas Report recounts a corporate culture that sought to pin responsibility on others and a Sisyphean search for the "root cause."

Further, even if the precise linkage between the ignition switch defect and moving stalls and airbag non-deployments was unclear, Old GM had enough knowledge. At minimum, Old GM knew about moving stalls and airbag non-deployments in certain models, and should have revealed those facts in bankruptcy. Those defects would still be the basis of "claims," even if the root cause (the ignition switch) was not clear.

New GM argues in response that because plaintiffs' claims were "contingent," those individuals were "unknown" creditors as a matter of law. But contingent claims are still claims, §101(5), and claimants are entitled to adequate notice if the debtor knows of the claims. Moreover, as discussed above, the only contingency was Old GM telling owners about the ignition switch defect—a contingency wholly in Old GM's control and without bearing as to *Old GM's* own knowledge. New GM essentially asks that we reward debtors who conceal claims against potential creditors. We decline to do so.

Finally, we address a theme in this case that the GM bankruptcy was extraordinary because a quick §363 sale was required to preserve the value of the company and to save it from liquidation. *See* New GM Br. 34 ("Time was of the essence, and costs were a significant factor."). Forty days was indeed quick for bankruptcy and previously unthinkable for one of this scale. While the desire to move through bankruptcy as expeditiously as possible was laudable, Old GM's precarious situation and the need for speed did not obviate basic constitutional principles. Due process applies even in a company's moment of crisis.

We find no clear error in the bankruptcy court's finding that Old GM knew or should have known with reasonable diligence about the defect. Individuals with claims arising out of the ignition switch defect were entitled to notice by direct mail or some equivalent, as required by procedural due process.

...

We address two further concerns. First, the bankruptcy court stated that it "would not have let GM go into the liquidation that would have resulted if [it] denied approval of the 363 Sale." In other words, the bankruptcy court suggested that it would have approved the §363 sale anyway, because the alternative was liquidation—and liquidation would have been catastrophic. While we agree that liquidation would have been catastrophic, we are confident that Old GM, New GM, Treasury, and the bankruptcy court itself would have endeavored to address the ignition switch claims in the Sale Order if doing so was good for the GM business. The choice was not just between the Sale Order as issued and liquidation; accommodations could have been made.

Second, many of the peculiar facts discussed apply with less force to the Non-Ignition Switch Plaintiffs, who assert claims arising from other defects. The bankruptcy court entered judgment against the Non-Ignition Switch Plaintiffs based on its opinion determining the rights of the other plaintiffs, but left as an open question whether Old GM knew of the Non-Ignition Switch Plaintiffs' claims based in other defects. Without factual findings relevant to determining knowledge, we have no basis for deciding whether notice was adequate let alone whether enforcement of the Sale Order would violate procedural due process as to these claims.

To conclude, we reverse the bankruptcy court's decision insofar as it enforced the Sale Order to enjoin claims relating to the ignition switch defect. Because enforcing the Sale Order would violate procedural due process in these circumstances, the bankruptcy court erred in granting New GM's motion to enforce and these plaintiffs thus cannot be "bound by the terms of the [Sale] Order[ ]." *In re Johns-Manville Corp.* (2d Cir. 2010). As to claims based in non-ignition switch defects, we vacate the bankruptcy court's decision to enjoin those claims and remand for further proceedings consistent with this opinion.

E. BREAK-UP FEES AND BIDDING PROCEDURES

F. CRITIQUING THE SALE ALTERNATIVE

> Add at the end of the Textual Note at pp. 747-750:

The Supreme Court in the following passage from *Czyzewski v. Jevic Holding Corp.*, 137 S.Ct. 973 (2017) drew a comparison between §363 sales and the unlawful "structured dismissal" before it that may suggest a level of discomfort with existing §363 sale practices:

"Rather, the distributions at issue here more closely resemble proposed transactions that lower courts have refused to allow on the ground that they circumvent the Code's procedural safeguards. *See, e.g., In re Braniff Airways, Inc.* (5th Cir. 1983) (prohibiting an attempt to "short circuit the requirements of Chapter 11 for confirmation of a reorganization plan by establishing the terms of the plan sub rosa in connection with a sale of assets"); *In re Lionel Corp.* (2d Cir. 1983) (reversing a Bankruptcy Court's approval of an asset sale after holding that §363 does not "gran[t] the bankruptcy judge carte blanche" or "swallo[w] up Chapter 11's safeguards"); *In re Biolitec, Inc.* (Bankr. N.J. 2014) (rejecting a structured dismissal because it "seeks to alter parties' rights without their consent and lacks many of the Code's most important safeguards"); *cf. In re Chrysler LLC* (2d Cir.

2009) (approving a §363 asset sale because the bankruptcy court demonstrated "proper solicitude for the priority between creditors and deemed it essential that the [s]ale in no way upset that priority"), *vacated as moot,* 592 F.3d 370 (2d Cir. 2010) (*per curiam*)."
137 S.Ct. at 986.

Shortly after *Jevic* was decided, Judge Christopher Sontchi found that *Jevic* precluded a settlement of creditor committee objections to a §363 "credit-bid" sale. Pursuant to the settlement, the buyer (an affiliate of the senior note-holders) had agreed to contribute estate causes of action it had acquired under the sale order back to a trust for the benefit of general unsecured creditors, without providing for higher priority administrative claimants. *See* Law360, *Jevic Ruling Scuttles Constellation's Ch. 11 Dismissal (In re Constellation Enterprises LLC et al., Case No. 1:16-bk-11213, U.S. Bankruptcy Court for the District of Delaware* (May 16, 2017)). Current Delaware §363 practice in Chapter 11 cases commonly involves credit-bidding secured parties making some provision for general creditors in order to overcome objections to the sale. Query whether *Jevic* will prove to be a general obstacle to such practices, resulting in more conversions to Chapter 7 (where committees do not generally play a role) and fewer bankruptcy sales in Chapter 11. The risk is greatest in cases in which there is insufficient value for the acquiring secured creditor, as the price of the convenience of the 363 sale process, to satisfy all priority claims *and* leave something for the unsecureds. In *In re Eternal Enter., Inc.,* 2017 Bankr. LEXIS 1027 (Bankr. D. Conn. Apr. 13, 2017), the court noted that *Jevic* had relied on early sale decisions such as *In re Lionel Corp.,* 722 F.2d 1063 (2d Cir 1983) that had disapproved sales that circumvented procedural safeguards for creditors in Chapter 11.

CHAPTER 13

THE BANKRUPTCY COURTS

A. ORIGINAL JURISDICTION

> At the end of Note 1 at p. 771 add the following:

In *Wellness International Network, Ltd. v. Sharif*, 135 S. Ct. 1932 (2015), the Supreme Court resolved one of the most important outstanding issues raises by *Stern v. Marshall*, finding that with the parties' express or implicit consent the bankruptcy court could constitutionally adjudicate a claim that would otherwise require district court action under *Stern*. *Wellness*, especially given the Supreme Court's prior Term's decision in *Executive Benefits Insurance Agency v. Arkison*, discussed at TENTH EDITION pp. 772-773, suggests that the Supreme Court majority wants the bankruptcy system to move past *Stern* and keep adjudicating cases more or less as it has done since 28 U.S.C. §157 was enacted in 1984 in the wake of its earlier thunderbolt, *Northern Pipeline Construction Co. v. Marathon Pipeline Co*. Even in dissent, Chief Justice John Roberts and Justice Clarence Thomas found ways in *Wellness* to ensure that the bankruptcy court's ruling could stand as a final judgment and no mere report and recommendation, in Roberts's case by adopting an expansive view of property of the estate, and in Thomas's by suggesting the existence of a brand-new fourth "bankruptcy" exception to the traditional trinity of Article III exceptions of courts martial, territorial courts, and matters of public right. All the *Wellness* opinions provide fodder for limiting the scope of *Stern* to, well pretty much to, §157. Of course issues remain, and there will be more *Stern* litigation. In bankruptcy cases, we continue to see more reports and recommendations and withdrawal motions than we were previously used to seeing. Procedures for handling them still need to be both elaborated and refined. There has been a diversion of some workload from Article I bankruptcy appellate panels (and to a much lesser degree, bankruptcy courts) to Article III district courts. But the workload shifts are not all that great, those bankruptcy court recommendations seem to be reviewed pretty much on the same basis as an appeal would be (albeit only after formally reciting the magic Article III words "de novo review"), and most of those withdrawal motions continue to be denied. *Arkison* ensures that a formal error in mischaracterizing a *Stern* claim as having been adjudicated by summary judgment in the bankruptcy court won't undermine finality at least so long as an "appeal" is taken. *Wellness*, by permitting an inference of consent from conduct to cure a *Stern* defect, limits the parties' ability to strategically manipulate the *Stern* rule. *Wellness* and *Arkison* both eschew the formalism of *Stern* and adopt functionalist perspectives to Article III to uphold pre-*Stern* practices. The Supreme Court majority does not seem to have any stomach for the enterprise of creatively re-imagining and then enforcing the notoriously opaque summary vs. plenary distinctions under the Bankruptcy Act of 1898, or eighteenth-century English bankruptcy commissioner-style limitations on modern bankruptcy court authority, as has been warned or feared, or in some cases, gleefully anticipated.

1. FURTHER LIMITS ON ORIGINAL JURISDICTION

    a. Withdrawal of the Reference

> Insert at the end of Textual Note on p. 776:

In a comprehensive nationwide empirical study of motions to withdraw the reference filed in FY 2013, Professor Laura Bartell found 253 cases in which such motions were filed (some cases involved multiple motions) representing about 1% of the total number of bankruptcy proceedings potentially subject to withdrawal. There were wide variations in the frequency of filing of these motions in various parts of the Nation with districts in California and Texas leading the pack. Fifty-eight percent of the motions were unopposed; overall (including both opposed and unopposed motions) seventy percent were granted in whole or in part. About forty percent of motions were in cases that implicated jury trial rights. Withdrawal for purposes of trial should follow as a matter of course if the jury demand is proper and all parties do not consent to a jury trial in the bankruptcy court. Laura B. Bartell, *Motions to Withdraw the Reference—An Empirical Study*, 89 AM. BANKR. L.J. 397, 410 (2015). The overall seventy percent success rate for withdrawal motions (including large numbers of uncontested matters and matters implicating jury trial rights) therefore suggests that the chances of successful withdrawal are quite low in non-jury cases that are contested.

B. VENUE

C. APPELLATE JURISDICTION

> In the Textual Note on p. 799 note the following matters:

The Supreme Court Reporter citation to *Bullard v. Blue Hills Bank* is 135 S.Ct. 1686 (2015). As the text suggested might well happen, the Ninth Circuit, citing *Bullard* in support and rejecting contrary suggestions in its own prior caselaw, has determined that district court or BAP remands of otherwise final bankruptcy court orders do not meet the standard of finality necessary to confer appellate jurisdiction on the Court of Appeals under 28 U.S.C. §§158(d), 1291. *In re Gugliuzza*, 852 F.3d 884 (9th Cir. 2017).

D. RIGHT TO JURY TRIAL

> Update the reference to *Wellness* in Note 4 following *Granfinanciera* at p. 813:

Wellness International Network, Ltd. v. Sharif, 135 S. Ct. 1932 (2015) found that the parties may waive Article III requirements in the context of a *Stern* challenge implicitly bolstering the constitutionality of 28 U.S.C. §157(e).

E. TRANSNATIONAL BANKRUPTCY